PAINTING ∘ COLOUR ∘ HISTORY

COLLECTION PLANNED AND DIRECTED BY

ALBERT SKIRA

SPANISH PAINTING

FROM VELAZQUEZ TO PICASSO

TEXT BY JACQUES LASSAIGNE

TRANSLATED BY STUART GILBERT

SKIRA

Copyright 1952, by Editions Albert Skira, Geneva (Switzerland).
Printed in Switzerland.

CONTENTS

THE COLORPLATES

OUR aim in the first of these two volumes on the History of Spanish Painting, *From the Catalan Frescos to El Greco*, was to throw new light on the Primitive Schools and in particular on some very remarkable Spanish artists whose individual genius had been all but submerged by the vast output of those prolific centuries. While in the present volume, the outstanding personalities of El Greco, Velazquez, Zurbaran, Goya and Picasso have, as is fitting, pride of place we also seek to bring out the background of their brilliant achievement. A great genius often gives the impression of a man born out of his due time and of owing little to the conditions of his age, and this holds good especially for Spain, by reason of the self-imposed isolation of so many of her famous artists. Nevertheless much may be gained by studying the historical setting of the personal ventures of the men of genius named above and their repercussions on the course of Spanish art ; thus we have also drawn attention to the work of other artists who, if less conspicuous, are very far from negligible. For great creations do not spring from nothing and a well-prepared soil is needed if the creative impulse is to yield its finest fruit. Moreover, though the highest honor falls to those who scaled the heights, it would be unjust to take no account of those whose commendable efforts tided Spanish art over the lean years and ensured its continuity.

The great Spanish painters have a forthrightness all their own ; they go straight to essentials and, even at the cost of a certain monotony, their approach is always simple and direct. Also, their refusal to conform is absolute ; neither official functions nor any outside pressure is permitted to restrict their freedom. Bathed in the magic light of a Velazquez or a Goya, themes are revealed in all their essential starkness and with an objectivity that is sometimes almost startling. Thus traditionally ' glamorous ' as a subject may be, we are left with no illusions. So keen is their vision that it pierces to the very core of reality. Every picture by these Spanish artists is unique of its kind and bodies forth a truth behind appearances. Doubtless there are other Schools which excel in decorative or didactic qualities, or sponsor aesthetic programs of a more sophisticated order, but none maintains a tone so finely balanced in dealing with passions keyed up to their highest pitch and with death under its grimmest aspects.

★

We wish to express our gratitude to all those who have contributed to the success of this book by permitting us to reproduce outstanding works of Spanish art in their keeping, and particularly to Sr. Gallego Burin, Director of Fine Arts in Spain, who, like his predecessor, the Marquis of Lozoya, has given us invaluable help ; to the Duke of Alba, the Marquis of Casa-Torres, the Count of Villagonzalo, M. Carlos de Beistegui, Count Contini-Bonacossi, Mr Oskar Reinhart, Mr Charles Im Obersteg, Mr Frua de Angeli, the Conservators of the Prado, of the Museums of Modern Art of Madrid and Barcelona, of the Louvre, of the National Gallery, London, of the Metropolitan Museum of Art, New York, of the Museums of Boston, Buffalo and San Diego, the Father Superior of the Monastery of Guadalupe, the parish priest of Santo Tomé at Toledo and the Rev. Father Superior of the Escuelas Pais de San Anton, Madrid.

EL GRECO

AND HIS AGE

RECO (1541-1614). THE BURIAL OF COUNT ORGAZ, 1586. (189 × 141¾")
CHURCH OF SANTO TOMÉ, TOLEDO.

8

EL GRECO AND HIS AGE

FOLLOWING an argument from analogy which was in high favor during the Middle Ages and, despite the objections raised by modern art historians, has something to be said for it, the historical evolution of the arts in social groups may in some respects be likened to the development of the artistic faculty in the individual. Certainly this analogy must not be taken over-literally or pressed too far ; we cannot expect it to solve the highly complex and sometimes baffling problems set by the evolution of forms in any given land or period. Nevertheless it can often be surprisingly helpful in elucidating some of them. Children have a natural gift for observing and grasping (even before they understand what they are seeing) the world around them and translating it into plastic terms ; and this they do effortlessly, in play. With the coming of adolescence this remarkable faculty (which all of us possess to some extent in childhood) tends to die out. The disciplines of education and also, no doubt, the normal processes of mental development cause an impoverishment of the child's sensorial perceptions, with the result that the growing youth begins to feel at a loss *vis-à-vis* his visual experience. He has lost that happy spontaneity and accessibility to impressions which enabled him in childhood to illustrate his perceptions or imaginings in a convincing manner and to impart apt, poetic, often quite fascinating overtones to even his clumsiest performances. It is a singular fact that at this later stage of his development, when his new-won intellectual powers mean so much to the young artist, he should tend to represent the world in terms of direct sensorial experience ; whereas in the earlier phase, when his intellect was in abeyance and his mental life ruled by emotive stimuli, he tended to visualize the world in terms of abstract formulas, from a quasi-intellectual angle. However, once through with the crisis of adolescence, the mature artist succeeds, by dint of slow and patient study of the real world, in shaking off the thrall of appearances and their unrewarding superficiality ; then, if at this stage he avoids the pitfalls of academicism and its formalized procedures, he may set to building up his personal language and perhaps win through one day to that spacious freedom which is the goal of truly creative genius.

The Primitives were not children. Often they possessed a knowledge of the *métier* superior to ours ; yet somehow they retained the attitude to art we find in children. There are Primitives in every age and clime ; even today we have our so-called naïve painters and they, too, are childlike. In actual fact the early painters we call Primitives belonged to a highly evolved stage of culture and functioned in a fully integrated art cycle ; they had a rare understanding of composition and many of the technical devices they employed have never been bettered. But the disciplines which ruled their art came wholly from within. They stemmed from the artist's spiritual outlook on life, particularly from his belief in the divine ordinance of the world. But this did not mean that the artist saw the world with the eyes of the average mediaeval Christian. Though the scope allowed the artist was often narrow and caprice could play no part in the creative act, he could none the less give rein to his sensibility and make proof of originality. Hackneyed as were the themes and however limited the artist's freedom, these primitive pictures opened up new vistas of the creative imagination and possibilities of almost endless variations ; we feel that the artist is revealing the inmost nature both of living beings and natural objects. The reason is, perhaps, that the Primitive felt himself posted at the heart of things ; forming part, that is to say, of a coherent cosmos and at one with it. But an ineluctable evolution, like that which leads the growing child towards a more literal rendering of his visual impressions, gradually led the mediaeval painter to abandon his overall conception of the picture and his expression of movement and life by those all-pervading rhythms and undulations, symbols of universal significance, which until quite recently seemed so baffling to the modern eye ; he now began to concentrate on details and their accurate rendering, with the result that the living, fully integrated form was replaced by the individual figure, to the detriment of life and movement; thus, thinking to progress, he in fact impoverished his art.

If it be granted that after the downfall of the Roman Empire the western world lapsed into a state resembling that of childhood, the Romanesque artists were like the child who interprets schematically what he sees. Indeed the course followed by their major works is both enlightening and typical. To start with, God the Father was never portrayed in person ; next, He was represented by a sign or an ellipse ; and finally by the aged man with whom we are so familiar. The other figures similarly ' aged.' Christ was represented at first merely by a cross ; then He became a young man wearing a robe ; then a man bearing the marks of age and suffering, and finally an all but naked figure treated with unflinching realism. Starting out from archaic forms containing what are certainly local survivals of Celtic or barbarian procedures, the Romanesque art of Catalonia introduced new signs, the shorthand notes as it were of facts of visual experience, into its vast decorations. Next, during a period of fruitful experimentation, we find an ever-increasing wealth of detail, and large-scale oecumenical composition came into its own. Meanwhile, however, the artists were growing more and more obsessed with realism and the subjects of their compositions (now transposed from the church wall to the altar) assumed more and more importance, became standardized and static, and were presented as separate pictures. Iconography triumphed over the cosmic vision and Gothic painting foundered in a jagged, crudely objective realism.

With its rationalism, its desire to base all knowledge on so-called scientific observation and its belief in human " progress," the Renaissance dealt its death-blow to the mediaeval concept of the world as a divinely organized whole. Turning their backs on the past, the men of the Renaissance did not hesitate to misrepresent the message of the Middle Ages and replace it by a new outlook on the world, clearer no doubt, more logical, but certainly less universal. Thus a barrier of incomprehension grew up between the past and the present and many centuries had to elapse before men re-discovered the true significance of the mediaeval world, too self-contained perhaps, but wonderfully coherent. Despite its brilliant achievements the Renaissance brought about a very real spiritual impoverishment. Artists thought to derive the basic laws of art from a knowledge of anatomy and the rules of perspective, and very soon they found themselves in a wasteland of neutral, impersonal forms, which had somehow to be peopled once again with living presences. By submitting to an *a priori* concept of the universe as a whole, the Primitives had been able to create truly original works ; whereas mere empirical observation led but to a frigid, classical beauty, lacking the breath of life. Indeed conventionality set in much sooner in that perfected universe built up with allegedly " ideal " aspects of nature, than it had in the symbolical or synthetic compositions of the Middle Ages. Thus the artist of the early seventeenth century resembled the man who, once the throes of adolescence have subsided, must cast about for new means of expression. Nothing remains of the heaven-sent gifts of childhood, he must fall back on his own resources, and in this deprivation he finds his best source of inspiration in contacts with the world around him.

Spain reacted in a very special way to the impact of the Renaissance ; indeed, being what it was, the Renaissance movement was little calculated to appeal to the Spanish temperament. Thus, whereas hitherto the primitive schools of Catalonia, Aragon, Navarre, Castile and eastern Spain had evolved on lines running parallel to those of Italian, Provençal, Flemish and Rhineland painting (though usually assuming original forms and distinguished by the power of their drawing) and, because the problems were the same, gave similar answers to them, the sixteenth century brought to an end this friendly dialogue between Spanish art and that of other countries. It was not that intercourse between them ceased, but that the tendencies of the Renaissance were uncongenial to the Spanish mind. The Spanish artist could never fall for the lures of an ideal beauty, existing in its own right, or the glamour of the naked body. Rather, he sought to overcome the flesh and torture forms into expressing the melancholy thoughts and dark forebodings inspired by his acute awareness of the human predicament. True, some Spaniards went to school with the Italian Masters and displayed great skill in imitating their techniques, but no sooner were they back in Spain than the

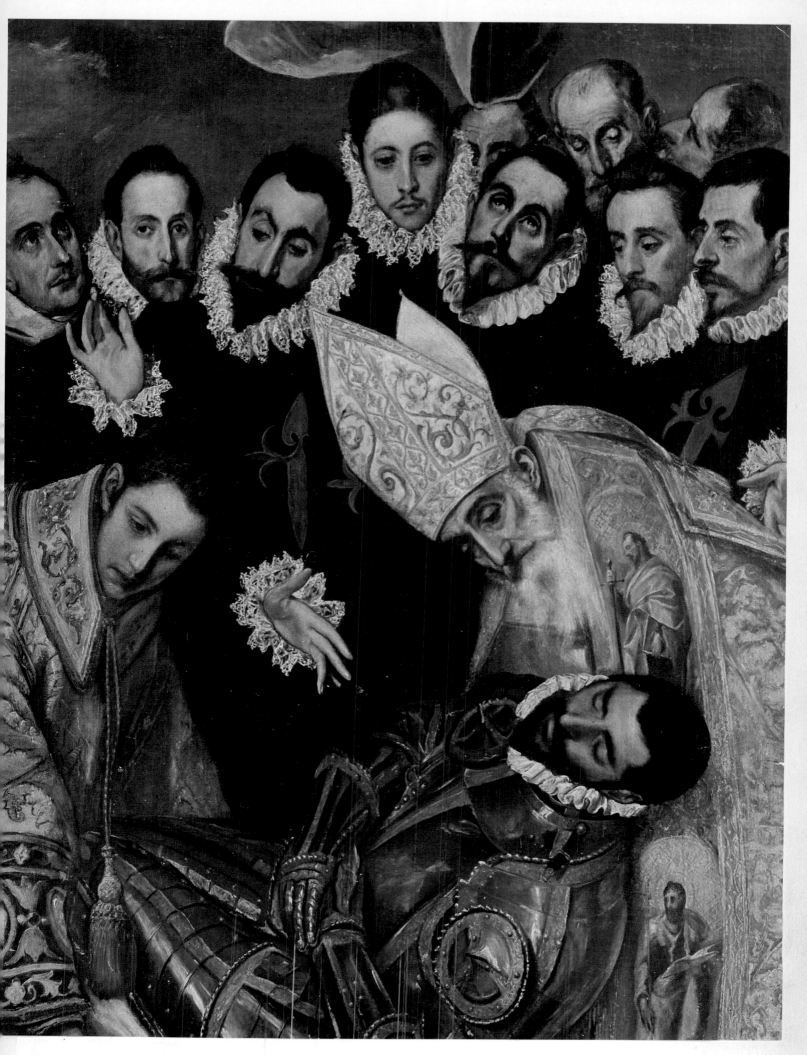

EL GRECO (1541-1614). THE BURIAL OF COUNT ORGAZ, 1586. DETAIL.
CHURCH OF SANTO TOMÉ, TOLEDO.

EL GRECO (1541-1614). THE BURIAL OF COUNT ORGAZ, 1586. DETAIL.
CHURCH OF SANTO TOMÉ, TOLEDO.

influences of their *milieu* prevailed. Thus Berruguete devoted his new-found technical proficiency to the service of a mysticism which, far from being tempered by humanism or Italian grace, gained in strength and fanatical intensity. The naïve procedures of mediaeval piety were not discarded but incorporated in a more solid composition, which made them more effective vehicles of religious instruction. Despite a weakness for the luscious modeling and emotionalism which were the commonest (and least commendable) elements of the heritage of Leonardo, the Hernandos avoided mawkishness thanks to their rustic vigor. This quality (which indeed persists throughout Spanish art) finds expression in the frequent use of broad planes laid out in cubes, which lend themselves to a pictorial architecture in terms of color and color contrasts, far more plastic than that resulting from the play of light and shade. Juan de Juanes did much to tone down the harshness which characterizes his father Vicente Masip's pictures, but not to the point of impairing the austerity of the elder artist's style. It was the rugged grandeur of Vicente Masip and not Juan de Juanes' suavity (though the latter served as a connecting link) that, along with the best Valencian traditions, took most effect on Ribalta and the new realistic Spanish school. Even the painters of Seville (of all Spanish cities, the most cosmopolitan and amenable to Dutch influences) who had been such fervent votaries of Italian methods, soon struck out on their own lines; indeed their native exuberance prevented them from enduring for any length of time a foreign yoke. Thus Pablo de Cespedes' exaggerations implement a strikingly dynamic lyricism; as we see in *The Last Supper* (Seville), in which the composition is thickly charged with anecdotal details, each given a value of its own, yet is pervaded through and through by a tempestuous rhythm due to the boldness of the drawing and clashes of the most unlooked-for colors. In this remarkable work, a milestone on the way to Valdés Leal's romantic visions, the distortions of the drawing and the vivid tonalities, defying alike the taste and sense of measure prevailing at the time, herald the coming of a quite new mode of expression. Even Pacheco, despite his deference to the canons of art, shows in the long succession of his portraits that he tended to study more and more the psychological make-up of his sitters and by the elimination of all non-essentials to override the conventions of the day. Though a number of Italian artists were summoned to Spain by Philip II for his big decorative projects, the mere fact that these artists worked in compact, exclusive groups prevented them from becoming acclimatized in Spain and negatived the influence they might otherwise have had on their environment.

It was largely due to its austerity and aloofness that sixteenth-century Spanish art escaped a peril threatening this most Catholic of countries more than any other. The Council of Trent, in which Spanish prelates played so large a part, had imposed on all Catholic countries an official iconography, proscribing all that was not historically authentic and vouched for by Holy Writ. The artist was expected to take orders from the theologian and devote himself to the promulgation of the doctrines of the Church and to the edification of his fellow-Christians. Clearly this pointed the way to a strict academicism, retaining only the more conventional and utilitarian elements of the discoveries of Leonardo, Raphael and Michelangelo—and, more than any other land, Spain seemed predestined to fall victim to a drab conventionalism. That she escaped this fate was due to the bold originality of her painters, to their aversion for over-generalized forms, and to an inner compulsion to solve for themselves the problems of art on more personal, more human, lines. And for this happy escape Spain owed most to the providential genius of El Greco.

Thanks to the commanding and compelling presence in its midst of " the Greek of Toledo " Spanish art, instead of remaining shackled in provincial forms—excellent no doubt, but cramping—was confronted with dramatic suddenness by the boldest innovations of the day : innovations which, as it so happened, stemmed no less from the remotest origins of Spanish art, which now, once more, was hearing the voice of the immemorial East, than from the logical, enlightened humanism of Western thought. El Greco brought to Spain the technical discoveries and all that was best in recent Italian art, combining the splendor that was Venice with the fine flower of Roman Mannerism. His wholly personal execution

EL GRECO (1541-1614). PORTRAIT OF FRAY HORTENSIO FELIX DE PARAVICINO, CA. 1609. (24¾ × 20½″)
COLLECTION OF THE MARQUIS OF CASA TORRES, MADRID.

breathed new life into the outworn procedures of the past ; born in the climate of Byzantium, he was alive to the advantages of well thought-out, coherent systems, but no less aware of the deadening effect of the set rules from which he had hastened to break free. Proudly conscious of his genius, he took from others what served his turn, only to pass it through the crucible of his creative imagination. Indeed when we look carefully into his art we find in it a complex of contemporary discoveries, assimilated, tested out and sublimated to their maximum emotive potency.

EL GRECO (1541-1614). PORTRAIT OF AN UNKNOWN MAN, CA. 1600. (18 × 17″)
PRADO, MADRID.

Moreover El Greco displayed a remarkable broadness of mind as regards the past;
he had a profound sense of the community of cultures and the permanence of certain values.
Architecturally minded, he believed in the necessity of an overall compositional order and
his art links up with the vast cosmic conceptions of the Middle Ages. He had too subtle
a mind to succumb to the glamour of a mythical "progress" destined to liberate Man and
make him the center of the Universe. In his work we have what Blake might have called
" A Marriage of Heaven and Earth " ; humanity is in close touch with the Other World, while

an observant deity arbitrates men's hopes and fears of an after-life. Thus, however other-worldly, his compositions are never inhumanly aloof; they borrow from the world of flesh even its decompositions, while dispensing with any purely material resemblance. Between the basic structure of the world of reality and that of the supernatural there is an underlying unity, and in almost all El Greco's large-scale works we find an atmosphere in which the two worlds merge harmoniously. Indeed, as has often been observed, it would be impossible to separate them in any of his works without producing an effect of mutilation. Perhaps the most perfect example of this interlocking of the transcendent and terrestrial worlds is *The Burial of Count Orgaz*; any isolation of the lower part of the picture (as, for example, in the early copies of Jorge Manuel and in some modern photographs) is obviously erroneous. All the more so because the fusion of the two worlds can be felt on every level of the composition; we perceive it not only in the etherial figures of the saints mingling so naturally with living men and in the gaze directed heavenwards of the mourners, but also in the presence at the center of the picture of that half-human, half-celestial personage, St John the Baptist, the mediator elect, proffering to God the earthly image of the miracle.

Yet, even in his most subjective creations, El Greco never fails to implicate a sort of objectivity, a so to speak concrete referent. The more he sublimates his forms, the more precise are his allusions to the real world around him. The period of his great *ensembles* was also that in which he made a great many portraits and these do not reveal a different trend of his creative impulse but the quest of a like truth. The reason why this part of his *oeuvre* strikes us today as the most 'modern' is that it reveals more simply, at its initial stage, the functioning of an interpretation of forms which, in the portraits no less than in the big compositions, engages the inner as well as the outer strata of the artist's conscious-ness. These faces, which so often owe their expressiveness to a few essential brushstrokes, strike us as wonderfully alive; but in them there is more than a rendering of outward appearance. Many are wholly imaginary; the artist has conjured up visions of persons who are dead; of whom he can have had only the dimmest recollection; or whose faces he knew only through inferior portraits. And he imparts to them a visionary life, fuller and truer, and on a loftier plane, than that of the men they were on earth. We need but compare this part of El Greco's output with the great Venetian school of portraiture (of which it is the logical outcome) to see the profound difference between them. Titian's and Tintoretto's portraits are magnificent, self-sufficient syntheses; they show their models as grandiose, soli-tary figures, stamped by their human destiny. Whereas there is a curiously haunting quality in El Greco's portraits; these people seem poised midway between life and death. Living as he did outside official circles and the royal court, El Greco painted for the most part men he liked or with whom he felt a spiritual kinship; we feel this in every one of his portraits. He aimed less at a *résumé* of his models' features than at plumbing the depths of their personalities—and, very likely, his own as well. Hence the 'family likeness' of all these faces, strongly individualized though they are. Immanent in all alike is the mind of El Greco himself, his insight, his philosophy of life, his rankling dissatisfaction, no less than his wayward fantasy; and it is this that gives them their intensity and their curious fascination. I question if any earlier painter ever revealed himself so wholly in his portraits.

In these works we see all the idiosyncrasies of El Greco's technique, and in them we also see how he preserved whatever was best in the past, while boldly opening portals of discovery. Color was for him a vital ingredient of design and pictorial architecture; thus he puts it to the service of his inner compulsions, without regard to natural appearance. If he preferred the cold palette of the Mannerists to the glowing, richly blended hues of Venice, this was because he realized the efficacy of pure, unbroken colors and the superiority of the effects produced by their juxtaposition. Moreover, though he often uses large, uniform planes, they never have the glossy, dead appearance given them by the Mannerists. He treats them merely as foundations (often laid in in tempera) on which to superimpose the touches of pure oil color which give vibration, life and movement to the picture surface. His contemporaries (as we learn from Pacheco) were surprised, indeed shocked by these

methods, seemingly so incompatible with the current view of 'finish' as a *sine qua non* for the picture. But the poets, Paravicino in particular, knew better ; they saw that by assuming different aspects when viewed close-up or at a distance enabling 'optical mixture' to take effect, the work of art acquired not only so to speak a greater flexibility, but was actually truer, better adjusted to the spectator's vision.

Similarly there is nothing 'classical' in his manner of locating forms in Space. Good Byzantine that he was, El Greco regarded painting as essentially an art of surfaces, and eschewed procedures giving the illusion of volumes—indeed any sort of pictorial illusionism. He suggested depth by the distortions he imposed on objects, while his elongation of forms was determined by the vanishing point, which he generally set as low as possible.

Thus, coming on the scene at a crucial phase of the transition from the conceptions of the past to those of the modern world, El Greco embodied in his work at once a restoration of the great traditions of a previous age and pregnant anticipations of the art of the future. During the same period Cervantes was summing up a whole civilization in an immortal work which, after beginning as a light-hearted satire, culminated in an epic of the impossible. Though it has not the rich complexity of Cervantes' masterpiece, El Greco's *oeuvre* can stand beside it. His influence made itself felt long after the age whose art his work so brilliantly outdistanced ; but for him the great discoveries of Velazquez (who was born in the year *Don Quixote* was published) would have been unthinkable ; indeed Velazquez' debt to El Greco can hardly be over-estimated.

EL GRECO (1541-1614). KNIGHT WITH HIS HAND ON HIS BREAST, CA. 1583. DETAIL. PRADO, MADRID.

THE SPIRIT OF TOLEDO

★

RIBERA: REALISM—AND BEYOND

ZURBARAN, OR PURE PAINTING

REVIVAL OF THE PROVINCIAL SCHOOLS

MURILLO: SENTIMENT AND SUAVITY

DIEGO VELAZQUEZ (1599-1660). THE WATER-CARRIER OF SEVILLE, 1618 OR 1620. DETAIL.
COLLECTION OF COUNT CONTINI-BONACOSSI, FLORENCE.

THE SPIRIT OF TOLEDO

WE are too apt to regard the work of a great painter as something standing alone and without posterity, the reason being that the disciples seem so sadly inferior when we compare them to the master. Actually this is seldom true, and it is especially untrue as regards El Greco. That meteoric genius could not flash across the Spanish sky without setting up long-lasting vibrations, and we are now beginning to discover that, despite the quite exceptional nature of his message, his direct influence was much wider than used to be supposed. Though he himself rarely left Toledo, his works were to be found outside the frontiers of the Province ; moreover many front-rank artists belonging to various schools, or associated with them, turned to him for guidance. In fact instead of speaking of a School of Toledo, we would do better to speak of a *spirit* of Toledo that made its presence felt in much Spanish painting of the early XVIIth century.

El Greco's most famous disciple, Luis Tristan, worked with him for at least four years (from 1603 to 1607), and though dying young (in 1624) left a copious *œuvre*. While keeping to El Greco's themes, he simplified the composition and scaled down the poetically exalted forms of the master to a closer approximation to reality. Thus even when the elements of the picture were the same, this difference of vision imparted to them a touch of almost homely realism, still very rare at the time. Tristan's art keeps nearer to the earth and his subdued colors, lacking the celestial translucency of El Greco's, accentuate this reversion to the humble realities of life. In his cold, meticulously precise portraits he confines himself to rendering externals, and produces austere, unrevealing effigies of his models. Though the old tradition that there were contacts between Tristan and Velazquez in his early youth is now regarded as highly dubious, this legendary association of the two artists' names testifies to the fact that the Sevillians were much interested in the art of El Greco and his followers : a fact that is further demonstrated by their purchases of the works of many Toledan painters and Pacheco's pilgrimage to El Greco's studio.

It was Pedro Orrente who ensured contacts with the Schools of the East. Born in Murcia round about 1570, he worked at Valencia before settling at Toledo. He became friendly with El Greco, and later was godfather of Jorge Manuel's daughter. Orrente made frequent trips to his native province, where he was given many commissions and exerted an influence sometimes rivaling Ribalta's. Best of his pupils was Estaban March, a painter gifted with no little *brio*, but whose style suffers from being too composite. During his Valencian phase Orrente had thoroughly mastered the procedures of the *tenebrosi* and he employed a palette of low-pitched, muted tones in his scenes of rustic life, rendered with a quiet matter-of-factness. His drawing has a fullness anticipating that of Ribera, while his composition is based on an interplay of simplified but strongly modeled volumes. This is what differentiates his art from that of the Bassanos, to which it is sometimes compared because the artists treat the same themes. As against the vibrant color orchestration of the Italians, Orrente uses neutral, unemotional tints, which reveal the subject in its essential starkness, while each detail tells out independently, given its full weight and value. It is an interesting point that on his visits to Cordova and Seville, Orrente won many admirers in these cities.

A progressive humanization of sacred subjects was taking place simultaneously at Valencia, in Ribalta's art ; at Toledo in the art of El Greco's followers ; and at Seville in the early work of Velazquez and Zurbaran. At this time Ribera's pictures had not yet found their way to Spain, and wherever Italian influences were felt they sponsored art trends much previous to Caravaggio. Thus the work of Fray Juan Bautista Mayno, who was born near Milan and whom we hear of as being in 1608 at the Convent of San Pedro Martir at Toledo, was still in the tradition of Orazio Gentileschi. An artist of unsure taste and often over-emphatic, he imparted to his colors a peculiar stridency and by using violent contrasts was able to dispense with shading. However, his composition and vigorous drawing affiliated him to Tristan, and he, too, was an austere portraitist. A little later in his career he took

FRAY JUAN SANCHEZ COTAN (1561-1627). BODEGON, CA. 1600-1601. (25½×32″)
FINE ARTS GALLERY, SAN DIEGO (CALIFORNIA).

to painting scenes of contemporary history, including landscapes, in the spirit of Pacheco but with more spontaneity. Thus in the *Reconquest of the Bay of San Salvador* the theme is treated on a human plane ; Mayno obviously enjoyed painting an episode that meant much to him personally. Though the Florentine painter, Vicente Carducho, had studied at Valencia and set up his studio in Madrid, he always remained a faithful follower of Tintoretto. A more famous artist, Roelas, likewise followed in the footsteps of the great Venetians and it was he (as A. L. Mayer has so well demonstrated) who, far more than Herrera the Elder, brought about the liberation of Sevillian art from the tedious convention-ality of Mannerism. Juan de las Roelas (or ' de Ruela ') was in Italy from 1606 to 1609, probably at Venice and at Parma. On his return he painted within a few years a series of gigantic works in various churches and in the Cathedral of Seville ; in these he combined the proportions of Michelangelo with the animation, the impetuous brushwork and brilliant color of the great Venetian decorators, and indeed they point the way to Rubens. This excellent painter had many pupils ; amongst them Varela and Juan del Castillo who was both the discoverer of Alonso Cano's talent and teacher of Murillo.

But undoubtedly it is Cotan who interests us most today. Long dismissed as a minor painter, he can claim to be regarded as an authentic pioneer, since he initiated the procedure followed by Velazquez, Zurbaran and even Murillo in their early works, of getting down

to the hard core of reality, at once dispensing with all so-called 'realistic' trivialities and disdaining the behests of an imaginary or ideal beauty. Born in 1561 at Orgaz in the old Castilian province of La Mancha, Juan Sanchez Cotan studied under Blas del Prado at Toledo. He began by painting 'bodegones,' and under his brush these still lifes of vegetables, fruit and game, then coming into fashion in so many countries, developed a completely new style and accent. Instead of striving to produce an effect of sumptuousness and to hold the eye by a crowd of objects closely juxtaposed, Cotan spaces them out on his canvas and by their isolation in space makes each of them tell out with its maximum intensity. Cotan became a monk relatively late in life (1604) and entered the Del Paular Carthusian monastery. We next hear of his presence at Granada in 1612. While continuing to paint his bodegones, he now undertook a large-scale religious work, whose simplicity and balanced composition are no less impressive. He took for his theme the most striking episodes in the annals of the Order, illustrating the fortitude of its martyrs in the face of persecution. In his big picture of the English Carthusians facing their judges, a lifted curtain discloses one of those architectural vistas, flooded with white, tranquil light, which were to figure in Zurbaran's masterpieces. Towards the close of his life he kept in close contact with the Sevillian painters, Roelas in particular. He died in 1627, at Granada. In that age of transition when even the most loftily inspired artistic ventures tended to lapse into theatrical over-emphasis, Cotan's work is distinguished by its fine coherence and avoidance of the meretricious. It is not too much to say that Cotan was the only artist of the period who clearly pointed the way to the achievements of Velazquez and Zurbaran.

Thus El Greco's Toledo may justly be regarded as a point of junction between the new developments in art and the time-proved values of the past, where, at the beginning of the XVIIth century, there took form what may be called the common denominator of Spanish painting. This common denominator is a sober, prudently controlled realism; the subject, well defined by carefully precise linework, is rendered without any concession to sentimental effect, yet without banality; the painter sees it steadily and whole. Before having recourse to the procedures of chiaroscuro, in which expression is achieved by contrasts

FRANCISCO ZURBARAN (1598-1664). BODEGON, CA. 1633. (23 ½ × 42")
COLLECTION OF COUNT CONTINI-BONACOSSI, FLORENCE.

between the elements brought to the fore and those that are concealed, the artist begins by using a palette which, conditioned by the subject, runs no risk of playing it false. Hence the predominance of neutral tints which do not distract the gaze from the picture as a whole : those bistres, browns and greys which, some three hundred years later, were to be the favorite colors of the Cubists.

Such were the most fruitful discoveries that had been made by Spanish art at the time when Velazquez and Zurbaran started their careers ; such were the means at their disposal. There were still traces of foreign contributions ; but such Italian influences as persisted, belonging as they did to a much earlier age, were on the way to being supplanted by the Spanish painters' simple, forthright vision of reality.

RIBERA: REALISM — AND BEYOND

There has been much controversy about the influence of Caravaggio on the Spanish art of this period. Early writers always took it for granted, but some modern art critics have dissented from this view, maintaining that, chronologically speaking, it is quite untenable. It is argued the art of Caravaggio and even that of Ribera could not have been known until much later, while the fact that stylistic affinities with it can be traced in the work of the younger Spanish artists merely illustrates a truth familiar to the art historian: that at certain periods new ideas are ' in the air ' and painters living at great distances from each other, facing the same problems, light on the same solutions. No doubt, since the days of Navarrete and Ribalta, Spanish art had become inured to *tenebrismo*, and artists had sought to renew their vision by integrating the real world within their art. But surely it would be unjust, while recognizing the progress already made in this direction, to leave out of account the decisive forward step sponsored by Caravaggio and Ribera. In a monograph on this subject as yet unpublished, Juan Ainaud de Lasarte proves conclusively that works by Caravaggio found their way to Spain (if not to Seville) in the years 1616-1619, when Velazquez, Zurbaran and Cano were taking their first steps in art. He is convinced that, even if the works themselves were not to be seen at Seville, the more cultured artists and especially the members of the group frequenting Pacheco's studio must have known all about the great Italian painter's new procedures—a view that is confirmed by Pacheco's writings. Velazquez' earliest works, could we be surer which these were and date them more positively, might help us to clear up the problem. Though we often find in them themes and accessories in the Dutch tradition, they soon begin to show the imprint of Caravaggio's style and mannerisms. Nevertheless their technique is remarkably different from that of the Italian master : a fact which tends to support the theory that the influence of his ideas took effect before that of the works themselves. Velazquez' palette (like that of Zurbaran in his early days) is persistently light, and in this respect its antecedents would seem to have been purely Spanish. It was not until a little later and, to begin with, chiefly in his religious works, that he took to using darker colors, while imparting to them more body and a richer glow. This change, coming as it did at a time when the painter was in full possession of his means and had made good his personality, may quite likely be connected with the beginning of Ribera's influence in Spain.

We now know that Ribera's artistic career preceded that of Velazquez by only a few years. It used to be assumed that there was a difference of twelve years between them; however, with the discovery of Ribera's certificate of baptism, the gap has been reduced to eight years, and there was the same interval between the dates of their deaths. Both were precocious artists ; but unfortunately in Ribera's case all the pictures he painted before going to Italy have disappeared, indeed our acquaintance with his work begins only when it was relatively mature. And by this time Velazquez had already found himself as an artist. Thus the period when the evolution of the two artists ran parallel was somewhat brief. Both alike progressed from chiaroscuro towards a freer use of light, but thereafter their ways parted. It is something of a paradox that though Ribera seeks almost violently to

JUSEPE RIBERA (1591-1652). THE MYSTICAL MARRIAGE OF ST CATHERINE. DETAIL.
METROPOLITAN MUSEUM OF ART, NEW YORK.

make his presence felt in his art, he remains impersonal and keeps to the plane of generalities, while Velazquez, haughty and reserved though he is, puts more and more of himself into each successive picture. Hence the fact that his work gives an effect of constant development, whereas Ribera remains static, crystallized in a perfection which, for all its excellencies, seems today outmoded. Thus the commonly held opinion that Ribera was a pathfinder calls for serious reconsideration ; so far as he is concerned, that role more properly falls to Ribalta and, so far as Velazquez is concerned, to El Greco. In fact Ribera's *œuvre* should, rather, be regarded as a culmination. Needless to say, this does not detract from its value ; on the contrary, its homogeneity and fidelity to the artist's initial concept command our admiration. For this aggressive, almost savage revolutionary was, *au fond*, a great classical artist.

Ribera, who is believed to have come of a poor family, was born at Jativa. As a boy he went to Valencia and studied under Ribalta. He seems to have thoroughly assimilated the notions and technique of his master : his expert draftsmanship, his pursuit of a new style based on objective naturalism, and even his colors, particularly his reds and vivid yellows. When he left for Italy (at a so far undetermined date) he was certainly a highly competent painter in the Spanish manner. And such he remained until his death, though he never returned to Spain. This is borne out by his Italian appellation of " Lo Spagno-letto " (originally a facetious reference to his small stature : " the little Spaniard ") and also by his frequent practice of appending the word *Español* to his signature. His successive sojourns in Rome, Parma and Northern Italy enabled him to study the masterpieces of the Renaissance. In later days he told Jusepe Martinez that, much as he admired Raphael, Michelangelo and Correggio, his personal taste drew him to Caravaggio. But obstinate as he was, he probably sought to trace in his masters those qualities which he already possessed himself. We hear of his presence in 1616 at Naples, which became his permanent home. This was the turning point of his career ; one might almost say he found himself famous overnight. We must remember that Naples was the capital of a Kingdom under the Spanish Crown and administered by Spaniards. The artist enjoyed the patronage of the successive viceroys, the first of whom, the Duke of Osuna (who hailed from the province of Valencia), despatched a number of Ribera's pictures to his family in Spain. Thus his fame spread all over Spain and many of his compatriots came to visit him, amongst them Jusepe Martinez (in 1626) and on two occasions (1629 and 1649) Velazquez, who had been sent by the King to buy pictures for the Escorial. The Italians were no less enthusiastic ; the Academy of Rome welcomed Ribera in its midst and the Pope conferred on him the decoration of " the Order of Christ." His studio at Naples was crowded with pupils, who aped him—or frankly stole his ideas.

There is little doubt that the plethora of replicas and ' echoes ' of his work has had the effect of blunting our enjoyment of his *œuvre* as a whole. Thus, when seeking to appraise it, we must be careful to exclude all that is not directly from his hand. Happily Ribera's personality was strong enough to leave a distinctive imprint on all the paintings authentically and solely his ; moreover (and this is very rare in the case of Spanish painters) a large number of engravings of his work are extant and these enable us to identify and to date many of his pictures. Ribera's draftsmanship is scrupulously exact : he delineates what he sees, but only what he sees. Thus he never blurs the palpable plastic boundaries of forms, or suggests more than meets the eye. His small, vigorous brushstrokes reproduce line for line all the idiosyncrasies of a face : its wrinkles, every crease of the skin and its very grain, the exact ' feel ' of beards and hair. Standing out emphatically against deeply shadowed backgrounds, figures are bathed in a harsh light that accentuates every detail, while in the bright passages each individual brushstroke is perceptible and plays its part.

The effects of Ribera's self-imposed limitations are evident in his renderings of biblical characters, whom he depicts merely as elderly men or repentant women bearing the marks of age and commonplace privations. In handling non-religious themes, as in the sequence (also in the Prado) of pictures of the sages of classical antiquity, he shows much zest in delineating their ragged garments, and quaint accessories of science or erudition. Here,

JUSEPE RIBERA (1591-1652). THE BOY WITH A CLUB-FOOT, 1652. (64½ × 36¼″)
LOUVRE, PARIS.

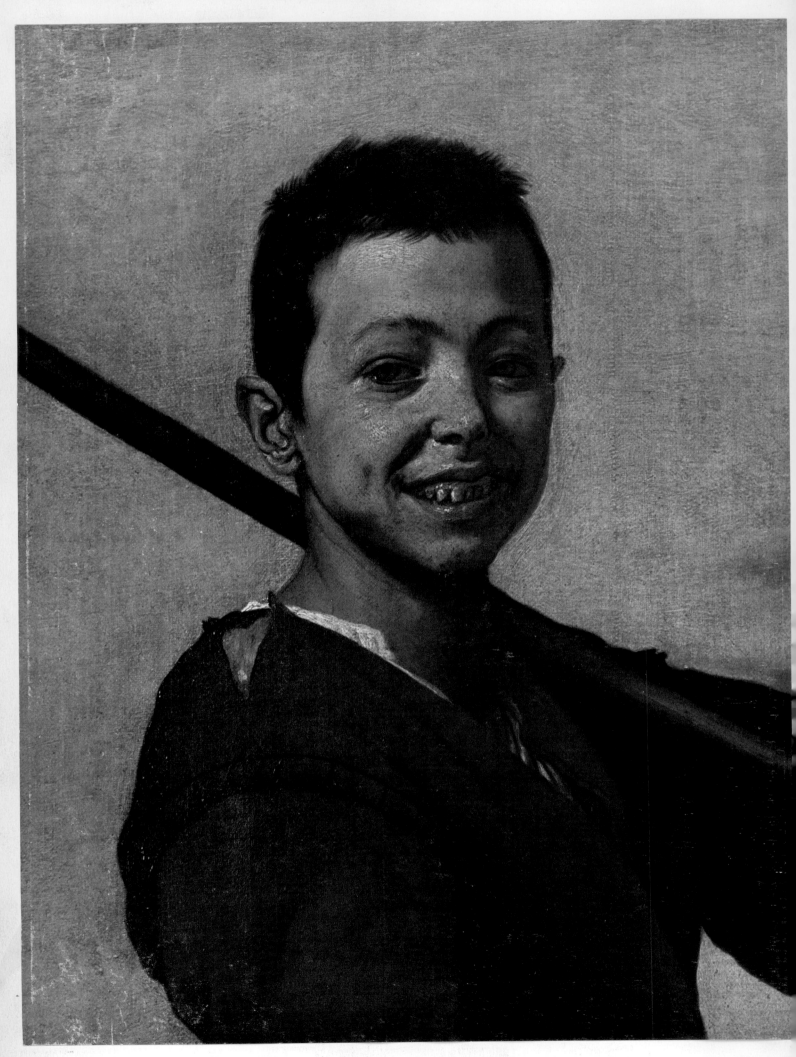

JUSEPE RIBERA (1591-1652). THE BOY WITH A CLUB-FOOT, 1652. DETAIL.
LOUVRE, PARIS.

DIEGO VELAZQUEZ (1599-1660). THE TOPERS, OR THE TRIUMPH OF BACCHUS, 1628. DETAIL.
PRADO, MADRID.

in fact, he betrays a lurking fondness for oddities and freaks of nature. His picture, named *La Barbuda*, of a bearded woman suckling a child (which is kept behind a curtain in the Tavera Hospital at Toledo), has something faintly sinister about it. The *Boy with a Club-Foot* (Louvre) on the other hand is one of his gayest works. Scenes of martyrdom were among his favorite subjects and, though these pictures have their admirers, their general effect is usually disagreeable, precisely because of the triviality of the ' horrors ' they record. In fact, in the case of beings so obviously lacking in any spiritual endowments, their sufferings are meaningless, all this wanton gruesomeness disgusts rather than appals us, and to differentiate the victims from their torturers, the painter has had to multiply grimaces.

It is different when death has brought peace to the tortured limbs, and in such cases we can admire Ribera unreservedly. For he can impart an accent of compelling truth when immobility or the poignant beauty of young bodies whence life has just departed is his theme. Thus the *St Sebastian* at the Valencia Museum and that of the Bilbao Museum, the *Dead Christ* of the National Gallery, London, and its counterpart at Naples, are among his most moving works. And, in the *Jacob's Dream* of the Prado, the mere fact that Jacob is dreaming seems to clothe him in an other-worldly light. Ribera's noblest figures are those which strike a note of pensive melancholy, such as the *Virgin* (Metropolitan Museum), or the Holy Woman with the red veil in the picture at Bilbao.

As the years went by a change came over Ribera's work ; the backgrounds became brighter, the colors warmer and lit with golden glints. The composition, too, to which massive shadows and stereotyped contrasts had imparted an excessive turbulence, grew less agitated now that light played a greater part, while his forms acquired a wonderful plasticity.

JUSEPE RIBERA (1591-1652). JACOB'S DREAM, 1639. ($70\frac{1}{2} \times 82\frac{3}{4}''$) PRADO, MADRID.

—   —

P.E. II 14

ZURBARAN, OR PURE PAINTING

Throughout the XVIIth century Spain had two great art centers, Seville and Madrid, to which in its opening years Valencia and Toledo had yielded pride of place. During this period, however, artists moved so freely and frequently from one center to another and from one province to another that any notion of local schools was by way of becoming obsolete. Thus the studio-schools which had flourished at the turn of the century, those of Ribalta, Pacheco, Roelas and even Herrera, had no equivalents in later years. Though there was constant intercourse with foreign countries, and especially with southern Italy, and though, as had already happened in the Middle Ages, artists throughout Europe were developing common tendencies pointing the way once again to an ' international style,' the effect of this concourse of influences on Spanish art was, paradoxically enough, to stress its Spanish characteristics. Moreover, so quickly did it come to maturity that after sponsoring, in the work of Zurbaran and Velazquez, creations that were at once fully integrated and perfect in their kind, it fell into a no less rapid decline, that made itself felt even in Zurbaran's last phase. None the less his works held their ground for many centuries, and indeed exerted an influence which gained strength as the years went by.

This flowering came so abruptly that one has the impression of a sudden revelation : the Spanish artists had at last found their appropriate language, and now, in full possession of their means, they felt impelled to set to work without a moment's delay. True, Velazquez went to Italy, but only in order to authenticate, as it were, the knowledge he already had abundantly. So vast was his culture that he was able to assimilate to a wholly personal (and national) idiom the most diverse artistic influences, whether these came to him through engravings or through contacts with originals. His world was founded on reality, in actual visual experience, and he submitted himself to it faithfully, almost humbly, even when he sought to body forth its most secret intimations. The case of Zurbaran was different ; his was a purely inner world, the fabric of a vision that took shape within him ; thus objective experience could but have distracted him from his self-communings.

Francisco Zurbaran was born in November 1598, a year before Velazquez, at Fuente-decantos, a hamlet in the Province of Badajoz, in Estremadura. His name suggests a Basque origin, like Goya's. In 1614 he was apprenticed for two years to an obscure Sevillian painter, Pedro Diaz Villenueva. His first signed canvases (1616) show a temperament that had already found itself at the early age of eighteen. Zurbaran did not frequent the famous studios of the city, but what he could have picked up from the great men of the day would probably have helped him little if at all ; neither the refined culture of a Pacheco nor the revival of the great Italian decorative tradition sponsored by Roelas was what he needed. No doubt he came in contact with these artists, but he felt on an equal footing with them. It was now that he became friends with Velazquez, then regarded by Sevillian dilettanti as the hope of the younger generation, and this friendship was to last throughout their lives, though from the start they followed very different paths, Zurbaran being the more sure of himself and the more self-willed, for all his modesty. When in 1629 he was commissioned to paint, in association with Herrera the Elder, the set of pictures illustrating the life of St Bonaventure, it was the older artist who seemed to rise above his ordinary self and draw inspiration from the style of his young colleague—anyhow as regards the composition ; for his execution still showed that almost frenzied straining after movement and those crude audacities which were the antithesis of all that Zurbaran stood for.

On some rare occasions, however, Zurbaran seemed to owe something to others. Thus, when in 1629 he was working on the huge pictures he painted at Guadalupe, he fell back on the procedures of the *tenebrosi* in dealing with the scenes figuring on a badly lit wall, and employed violent contrasts of light and shade, making vividly illuminated passages tell strongly out against dark backgrounds. Yet here, too, what was merely a procedure becomes under his brush the vehicle of a new expression ; this eerie world with its green dusk riven by sudden flashes of dazzling light, is a world of ' metaphysical painting ' in its

31

truest sense. At the close of his life, during that period of reduced output which has so much intrigued his biographers and may perhaps be explained by his chagrin at Murillo's rapid rise to fame, Zurbaran allowed a certain sentimentality to creep into his work and lost his personal accent; anyhow, there is no question that his powers were failing at this time.

For Zurbaran was not one of those happy few for whom the sheer joy of creation and their zest for life ensure a constant renewal of their youth. The tension permeating all his work was such that it could not last indefinitely. Indeed, so abstract and cerebral was his art, so allergic to any material referent or extraneous influence, that the painter could not hope to reinvigorate it by recourse to the real world. To begin with, there was a fusion of the mental and the physical which produced as it were a 'precipitate' in the artist's unconscious, and evoked images of the maximum intensity. And his hand registered these images with a fidelity that was nothing short of miraculous. Yet though the artist might deliberately seek after these emotive experiences and renew their effects, it was the expression of the first experience, the "first, fine rapture," that remained the most significant and the best. Repetition might purify, it could not enrich them, and 'progress' was ruled out. Once a painter like Zurbaran can no longer muster up the energy needed, his life's work is done. (Modern 'metaphysical painting' collapsed no less abruptly.)

In an achievement of this order material conditions count for little, and we need not be surprised that Zurbaran's private life escaped the limelight of publicity. His talent ripened quickly and, despite his early successes—notably in respect of his decorations in the Chapel of San Pedro and the Cathedral—he soon withdrew from the brilliant art world of Seville and settled, in or about 1625, not far from his birthplace, at Llerena, a small town in the heart of La Serena, a vast cattle-grazing area. There he married and had several children. He continued getting orders from Seville where such was his renown that in 1629, when he had only just turned thirty, the City Fathers invited him to return and take up his residence in Seville, promising him every amenity he could desire. This was the period when the great ecclesiastical Orders throughout Spain were commissioning cycles of pictures illustrating the glories of their past. Thus the set of pictures by Sanchez Cotan in the Charterhouse of Granada was made in 1625 and Carducho's *ensemble* for the Paular was painted between 1628 and 1638. The biggest commissions fell to Zurbaran. Of his work for the Dominican Convent of San Pablo, the admirable paintings in the Church of the Magdalen at Seville are extant, and he painted a series of pictures of the visions of St Peter Nolasco for the recently completed Convent of La Merced. Other works of this period are the scenes from the life of St Bonaventure, two of which are in the Louvre and another was in the Dresden Museum, and the set of pictures made for the Carthusian Monastery of Las Cuevas (now in the Museum of Seville) including *The Virgin Protectress of the Carthusians* and *The Miracle of St Hugo*. He also made the fine portraits of the Brothers of La Merced, now in the Academy of San Fernando, and (in 1631) the large *Apotheosis of St Thomas Aquinas*, now in the Museum of Seville, the work in which he approximates most closely to traditional classical composition. From 1633 onwards he was employed by the Carthusians of Jerez, for whom he painted his largest *ensemble*, including the four pictures in the Grenoble Museum and the scenes in the Cadiz Museum. Finally he painted (in 1638-39) a set of pictures for the Monastery of Guadalupe. All these great works were produced in a period of twelve years (1628 to 1640), and nowhere do we see the least trace of any flagging in the artist's inspiration; indeed it is amazing that he could maintain so high a standard through so copious an output. In 1640, however, Zurbaran entered on a period of great depression. His wife had just died and he re-married, had several children, and meanwhile commissions became rarer. Things came to such a pitch that he left Seville and went to Madrid, where Velazquez proved a friend in need. All the same, despite some tokens of royal favor, Zurbaran failed to mend his fortunes, one reason being that he was painting less and less. Except for some versions of *St Francis* and the two large pictures of Dominican monks in the Museum of Seville, he now produced only religious works of a commonplace kind. The *Christ Crucified with St Luke in the Guise of a Painter* (in the Prado), the 'St Luke' in

FRANCISCO ZURBARAN (1598-1664). THE VIRGIN AS A CHILD. (46 × 37")
METROPOLITAN MUSEUM OF ART, NEW YORK.

FRANCISCO ZURBARAN (1598-1664). THE REFECTORY OF THE CARTHUSIANS, OR THE MIRACLE OF ST HUGO,
CA. 1633. (103 × 125″) PROVINCIAL MUSEUM, SEVILLE.

which is thought to be a self-portrait, almost suggests that the painter has purposely keyed
down this picture to a studied coldness, devoid of any movement, the least breath of life.

The case of Zurbaran is quite exceptional in the annals of art; though antecedents
may be traced for some potions of his work, he had no masters. His still lifes may remind
us of Cotan, and certain old men's heads, such as the Seville 'St Peter' and the Guadalupe
'St Jerome' (in *The Temptation of St Jerome*), may recall those that recur so frequently in
Ribera's work, but intrinsically Zurbaran's art is all his own, he cuts a unique, solitary figure.
His training in art was of too rudimentary a kind to affect his melancholy, self-centered
disposition, and his work always bore traces of his peasant origins. The frequent variations
in his productivity show that his painting always stemmed from a deep but intermittent
urge to express himself. In his periods of unsureness he kept silence and there were occasions
when he so to speak 'went into retreat'; notably in his youth and after 1640. On the
other hand once the creative impulse seized him and he felt at one with the world, his
output was nothing short of prodigious. But when he was in a phase of deep depression,
as was the case at the end of his life, it seemed as if the elements of the picture refused to
fall into a pattern; hence the lack of balance and cohesion in his last works.

FRANCISCO ZURBARAN (1598-1664). ARCHITECTURAL VISTA: DETAIL FROM THE PORTRAIT OF
FATHER GONZALO DE ILLESCAS, 1639. MONASTERY OF GUADALUPE.

FRANCISCO ZURBARAN (1598-1664). SAN CARMELO, BISHOP OF TERUEL, 1629.
PROVINCIAL MUSEUM, SEVILLE.

FRANCISCO ZURBARAN (1598-1664). SAN LUIS BELTRAN, 1650.
PROVINCIAL MUSEUM, SEVILLE.

In a work by Zurbaran the subject has far less importance than the relations built up between forms. Indeed his themes are simple and little varied ; he contents himself with ringing the changes on them. Each personage is presented as an isolated unit, 'held' by the artist at the climax of his emotion or mystical experience. Details cease to count and can be disregarded ; thus the monks' faces are sometimes overshadowed by their cowls, without detriment to the expressive power of the figure as a whole. Hence Zurbaran's fondness for those long monastic garments, smooth blocks of whiteness, on which he can alternate planes of light and shadow, dappled with faint gleams of color. Enveloping the figure in a single movement, these garments produce an effect of overall integration, and upon this uniform ground he sometimes strews contrasting touches that enliven the surface. In these he shows a preference for bright colors: yellows, pinks and azure-blues for evocations of the celestial world, but also purples and violet-reds for the princes of the Church, and greens and vivid blues which tell out strongly beside passages of pure white. In fact he anticipates the modern view of the picture as " a flat surface to be covered with colors arranged in a certain order."

Zurbaran made no efforts to define or describe personalities; he rarely painted actual portraits. Rather, he created symbols, though giving them the weight and plenitude of living beings. In his numerous sequences of pictures illustrating the lives of saints, his indifference to the subject *per se* is obvious ; the figure is a ' build-up,' often highly complex and elaborate, of gestures swathed in gleaming fabrics.

Depth and perspective had little or no interest for him—though it is clear that he knew all about them. None the less in most of his major works we find an architectural background or vista, treated in a style so neutral and unemotional that it almost suggests a blueprint, and consisting of angles and perspectives bathed in a queer, crystalline dreamlight. This has nothing in common with the décors so often figuring in ' classical ' compositions from the Renaissance onward and of which Murillo, for instance, has given us some interesting examples. In his early work he places this architectural element outside the main composition ; of small dimensions, it suggests a miniature projection of the picture proper, a sort of vanishing point. In his later work the architectural features bulk larger (sometimes he even enlivens them with human forms) and we then can see their relevance : they correspond to the man who is portrayed, explain him and synthesize his personality. In fact they serve as windows opening on the spiritual world. The forms these ' windows ' take are often strange, the reason being that they stand for a psychic reality and their lay-out is not due to any geometric compositional scheme as is the case in Vermeer's pictures. In that wonderful portrait of *Father Gonzalo de Illescas* in the Monastery of Guadalupe, the scene beyond the room is treated with unusual fullness. It is framed between two dark pillars and just in front there is a still life of a book and an apple. The juxtaposition of such heterogeneous elements in an unexpected order and without regard to natural proportions stresses the impression of strangeness, almost eeriness, given us by a picture whose starting-off point is wholly conventional : a prior sitting, pen in hand, at a desk on which lie books and papers, and symbolical reminders of the vanity of all things human. The effect is to create unlooked-for correspondences, new associations in the mind of the spectator. It is this that gives the few still lifes that Zurbaran painted their striking originality; each object, displayed in an unwonted isolation and depicted with stark realism, keeps its magical power intact.

Now and then, in his second Guadalupe series (painted for the ill-lit side of the sacristy), the architectural elements are enlarged to the full dimensions of the picture and the figures move directly amongst them. Here their visionary quality is manifest ; they are quite unlike any of the religious edifices existing in Spain in Zurbaran's time, whereas there had been analogies with these in the background of the portrait of Father de Illescas. Since these pictures were to be hung in a bad light, Zurbaran made the most of the contrast between the black bands and the whites of the monastic habit, and faces are brilliantly illuminated. The painter's use of large, square planes is particularly effective in *The Farewell of Father Juan de Carrion*. *The Vision of Fray Pedro of Salamanca* is perhaps Zurbaran's most consistent work ; the whole composition is as it were a reflection of the prodigy that is taking

FRANCISCO ZURBARAN (1598-1664). ST DOROTHY, CA. 1640-1650.
PROVINCIAL MUSEUM, SEVILLE.

place outside the picture and whose supernatural effulgence, presaging the bloodshed and disasters of the Turkish invasion, casts a baneful glow upon the sky, the stones of the façade and even the eyes of the Brother and his companion.

In his inspired moments Ribera had occasional intuitions of that supremacy of plastic values which is unequivocally asserted throughout Zurbaran's *œuvre*. We need not be surprised by the fact that the full significance of this new development in art was not grasped by their contemporaries, who admired Ribera for his verism and expressionistic vigor and Zurbaran for his unrivaled skill in depicting monastic life and mystical emotion. Both painters, after attaining the pinnacle of success, outlived their glory and died all but forgotten. Yet surely a brilliant come-back, partial in Ribera's case and total in Zurbaran's, is overdue for both. For their work contains answers to the most urgent problems of modern art and they anticipated what is the chief concern of the artist of today: that of giving concrete form to creations of the mind. Thus Zurbaran ranks as a forbear of Cézanne, of Juan Gris' Synthetic Cubism and of Metaphysical Painting.

REVIVAL OF THE PROVINCIAL SCHOOLS

Long before his death Zurbaran gave the impression of having worked himself out. Already in the major achievements of his maturity—the *ensembles* at the Monastery of Guadalupe and the Carthusian Monastery of Jerez—there were hints of solipsism, his world was almost exaggeratedly self-contained. Only the works of his youth were in keeping with the spirit of his age. Thus the few disciples he had (amongst them José de Serabia, whose curious, realistic scenes of rustic life are now in the Museum of Cordova) always aligned themselves to his first manner. It is natural enough that there should be a sort of family likeness between the early efforts of Zurbaran, Velazquez and Alonso Cano, who were almost contemporaries ; but even Murillo, twenty years younger, drew his inspiration in his first phase from the same sources and in his early work there is a vein of naturalism.

Though Alonso Cano made a promising, not to say brilliant start, he failed to implement it fully, perhaps because he dispersed his creative energy, practicing decorative architecture and sculpture as well as painting. Nevertheless he played an important part in a transitional phase of Spanish art. A great traveler, he resided at one time or another in all the art centers, had many imitators and came in contact, though often only to attack them bitterly, with the best contemporary painters. He was born at Granada, where his father was a maker of the architectural framework of retables. Having joined Pacheco's studio, he was Velazquez' fellow-pupil, and soon made a great name for himself at Seville. A cantankerous, envious man, he protested against the appointment of Zurbaran, whom however he esteemed, as official painter to the City of Seville. When in 1638, probably on the recommendation of Velazquez, he was bidden to the royal court, he began to paint more boldly and had a share in the evolution of the School of Madrid. When in 1644 his wife was murdered under mysterious circumstances, he fell under suspicion and was imprisoned for a time ; after his release, he deemed it wiser to retire to Valencia. Next he went to Granada (after another stay in Madrid) and, despite incessant quarrels with the Chapter, executed some large commissions for the Cathedral of his native city before he died, in poverty, in 1667.

His arrogant, unstable temperament and the unusual combination of a wide culture with a readiness to try out new techniques assimilated Cano to the Masters of the Italian Renaissance. But he came too late into a world too old. And his achievement, uneven and fluctuating, fell short all too often of his grandiose intentions. During his first Sevillian period his painting is characterized by an emphasis on volumes, probably the result of his associations with sculpture ; in any case Pacheco was already encouraging his pupils to pay special attention to their modeling. Boldly illuminated, his figures stand out in remarkably strong relief ; thus the *St Inez* (Berlin Museum), perhaps his masterpiece, has a statuesque majesty and a pure beauty that are sometimes lacking in similar works by Zurbaran. His Virgins, too, have a monumental dignity all their own. His art being easier to grasp than Zurbaran's, it was

natural that his influence made itself felt more readily. While Cano was in Madrid, his tendency towards the 'humanization' of sacred themes gained impetus, though without impairing the overall dignity of his work. But his contacts with Velazquez brought a change; his painting grew more suave, while his palette grew richer; he now went out for 'effects,' and dappled his colors with brilliant, silvery gleams. Also, his composition became more Baroque, less formal; emotion and even humor (as in his *Goth Kings*) began to play a part in it. Though again, in his last phase, he harked back to purely painterly considerations as the dominants in his art, it was its emotive qualities that had most effect on those around him. A very active provincial school was flourishing at Granada, and Cano won some disciples, most fervent of whom was Pedro Atanasio Bocanegra (who later made a portrait of his dead master), a painter of a poetical turn of mind whose dramatic fantasies rank beside those of Valdés Leal and sometimes indeed excel them, so daring are this artist's flights of fancy.

To this much gifted generation whose emergence synchronized with the turn of the century belong also the Valencian Jeronimo Jacinto Espinosa and an Aragonese painter, Jusepe Martinez. The former, who studied under Ribalta and painted scenes of monastic life, has sometimes been described as "the Zurbaran of Valencia." But though he used tenebrist procedures to excellent effect, his depictions of the mystical experience lack insight and are merely superficial; as for his composition, what strikes us most is its wealth of brilliant ornamentation. A writer as well as a painter, Martinez is known chiefly for the visits he paid Ribera in Italy, and as the author of a treatise, *Manual of the Most Noble Art of Painting*. Published only in 1866, this work supplies much valuable information about the artistic activities of his day. It was, moreover, thanks to Martinez that the discoveries of the Schools of Seville and Valencia, and the advanced art of Italy, were made known in Aragon. Sponsored by Antonio Martinez, Jusepe's son, and that highly strung poetic painter Pablo Rabiella, a successful school was soon to arise at Saragossa. Thus all the provinces of Spain were quickly affected by the deep-seated changes, little short of a Renaissance, that were taking place in Spanish art.

These changes were speeded up by an influence that, stemming from abroad, had a far-reaching effect on the second generation of XVIIth-century painters, which included Murillo, Antonio del Castillo and Valdés Leal. This influence was Flemish. When Rubens came to Spain his vast prestige lent weight to the advice he gave Velazquez, and soon he had some almost servile imitators, such as Miguel Manrique (who worked at the Cathedral of Malaga). But it was on Van Dyck's work that interest seems to have centered. An old tradition has it that the first to draw inspiration from him was a Granadan artist, Pedro de Moya, one of Murillo's fellow-students in Juan del Castillo's studio and a friend of Cano and Bocanegra. It is said that Moya went to the Low Countries with the Spanish army and was so much impressed by what he saw of Van Dyck's work, that he contrived to cross to England where he attached himself to Charles I's painter-in-ordinary and worked with him for six months, making a great many copies which ultimately found their way to Seville. There is much doubt about the attribution of works reputedly Moya's, but Flemish influence is unmistakable in many Andalusian works of the second half of the century.

Antonio del Castillo, a Cordovan and nephew of Murillo's teacher, is one of the most interesting personalities of this second generation. He locates his Old Testament scenes in agreeably composed landscapes, abounding in picturesque details, men counting sacks of wheat, a cottage, a herd of cattle and the like, treated on thoroughly painterly lines. His desire for historical accuracy and his slightly naïve reminders of the exotic setting of the biblical legends did not prevent his depicting in these pictures quite ordinary people, posing them realistically and making them move naturally. The Cordova *Baptism of St Francis* is an unpretentious scene of family life, with, in the foreground, some young children forming a charming group in quite the XVIIIth-century manner. In some ways this work recalls Murillo at his best. Indeed it has perhaps more self-confidence, though it lacks Murillo's sweep and verve. None the less, the numerous drawings by del Castillo that have come down to us show that he was capable of vehemence as well as being a highly proficient draftsman.

BARTOLOMÉ ESTEBAN MURILLO (1618-1682). SAN DIEGO OF ALCALA IN ECSTASY.
DETAIL FROM THE ANGELS' KITCHEN, CA. 1645. LOUVRE, PARIS.

MURILLO: SENTIMENT AND SUAVITY

During his lifetime Murillo was praised to the skies and the contemporary estimate was endorsed by the international picture-market during the XVIIIth and XIXth centuries. The disrepute into which he so abruptly fell some fifty years ago strikes us today as overdone, nor does he lack defenders who draw attention to the sterling qualities of his art and his fine technique. In Murillo's case it is not only a matter of separating the works that are certainly by his hand from those whose attribution is questionable. For amongst the works authentically his many of the most popular strike the modern eye as quite intolerably mawkish and lacking in real substance. These are the pictures in which he exalts the more ingratiating aspects of religion at the expense of its stern realities, and reduces sacred subjects to agreeable scenes in which a group of sentimental personages, with tears in their eyes, gaze tenderly at a Child Jesus dressed up as a conventional shepherd. This is all the more odious because Murillo was capable not only of a vigorous realism but also of genuine religious emotion. But he is all too apt to lapse into a *confusion de genres* and sometimes into foolish over-statement. On these occasions he has recourse to gesticulations obviously out of keeping with his naturally contemplative turn of mind. The keynote of his character would seem to have been a very sincere piety, his refuge from a world he always found distasteful and the sense of loneliness resulting from his wife's death. His life was a series of frustrated hopes, one of them (according to biographers) being that of becoming a priest, and another that of visiting the fountainheads of art in Italy and Flanders. Actually it is doubtful if he even got as far as Madrid, so difficult did he find it to tear himself away from his work. He left a vast number of paintings and though using the same themes over and over again, never shows signs of lassitude. Indeed Murillo seldom repeated himself, he had a wonderful knack of varying his settings and the overall movement of his compositions.

In his numerous *Immaculate Conceptions*, each of which has a charm peculiar to itself, the central figure seems lifted high above all earthly contingencies by the swirling movement of a company of angels and the buoyant clouds; the Virgin has an august serenity, a sublime purity, in which we seem to have an echo of Cano's sober treatment of religious themes. Nevertheless she is a flesh-and-blood young woman, though built up as it were on classical lines by a synthesis of all the elements of ideal beauty. Thus Murillo created a special type of woman, who appears again and again in his portrayals of the Madonna and female saints. The face is exquisitely modeled, the hair, brown or black (one of his Virgins is known as ' The Gipsy Virgin '), frames it harmoniously, while the liquid, dreamy eyes seem fixed on the spectator. In *The Virgin of the Rosary* (Prado) the Child is rendered in the same manner and with no less dignity. This, a happy exception, is one of Murillo's best and most self-consistent works. For, all too often, the children in his pictures have an anecdotal quality that jars on us. On the other hand, in his cherubs and the purely decorative figures, which are not intended to ' tell a story ' of any kind, we find an admirable freedom in the execution and they are wholly charming.

In considering Murillo's art we come up once more against the problem of 'realism.' As we saw in the case of Ribera, naturalistic depiction can be a means of imparting an afflatus of real life to the dry bones of classically conventional compositions. But always the realistic painter runs the risk of limiting himself to a form of reproduction that is primarily anecdotal or sensational and thus unlikely to have any lasting value. To avert this, he tries to force a significance which they do not and cannot possess upon his ' snapshots ' of reality—the result being a convention far more deleterious than the classical convention. When he paints beggars, street urchins eating fruit or scratching themselves, Murillo avoids this pitfall; he aims at realism pure and simple, without any afterthought. His technique and his handling of contrasts and light effects are superb, though we cannot fail to recognize that his work in this field falls short of the similar work turned out by the young Velazquez thirty years before dand with fewer technical resources. Skillful and entertaining as it is, this part of Murillo's output just misses true significance. Indeed he comes dangerously near the ' genre scene' which for all its claims to be 'a slice of life' was not only one of the dreariest of conventions but the farthest from reality.

Murillo's best work was produced at the two extremes of his career. In his early days, when influenced by Ribera and the young Sevillian masters, Zurbaran and Velazquez, he painted the set of pictures for the Franciscans amongst which are his *Charity of San Diego* (Academy of San Fernando) and the *Angels' Kitchen* (Louvre). In the first-named picture he frankly kept to the neutral tints employed by Velazquez in his earliest phase. In the central portion of the composition, which consists of a number of children in prayer, the children gathered around a dish of food are painted with delightful simplicity and the painter in his rendering of the saint has not yielded to the obvious temptation to sentimentalize his subject. Some gaunt, uncouth figures of peasants and poor people stand out from the shadows on the periphery. The composition of *The Angels' Kitchen* shows much more arbitrariness, with its successive planes more or less linked up with each other : a group of visitors on the left (in which we see premonitions of the portraitist-to-be), then the saint in ecstasy, swept upward from the earth in an ascensional movement which at once dislocates and stiffens him ; and, finally, the angels and the magnificent still life of the utensils. Here the impasto is full-bodied and the color lit with warm, golden gleams.

When, years later, Murillo reverted to similar themes in painting his *St Elizabeth of Hungary* and *Charity of St Thomas of Villanueva*, a far-reaching change had come over his art. The emphatic outlines and solid volumes he had inherited from Cano had given place to fluid forms dissolving into a misty aura. These were more in keeping with the contemporary taste and have a sort of 'period' elegance. Beside Murillo's traditional beggars rendered with an impersonal naturalism we have more individualized and graceful figures, young girls whose slender grace and shimmering costumes of translucent grey remind us of Van Dyck and the Dutch Little Masters. Thus *The Virgin, Child and St Anne*, like Antonio del Castillo's little page-boys, already prefigures the art of another century.

In a still later work, the scenes of *The Prodigal Son* and a curious version of the tale of Joseph and Potiphar, these northern influences are still more pronounced. And here we are reminded of Rembrandt and his gnarled, stunted forms, though Murillo lacks his gift of molding his medium into creatures compact of passion and feverish unrest. The characteristics of his work are, rather, a gentle romanticism tinged with melancholy. The portraits of his last phase reveal an interesting re-interpretation of the methods of Van Dyck. The expressiveness of these tall, full-length, stooping figures, stems from a concentration and diminution of the features as against the elongation of the body. Also, a slight darkening of the face contrasts with touches of dazzling whiteness in certain details of the costumes—stockings, ruffs, the slashes of the sleeves and shirt-frills—which thus acquire a heightened significance.

Murillo's art, so fluid and so changeful, with its delicacy of color, its technical versatility and imaginative elegance, fell perfectly in line with a period of transition, and covering as it did considerable ground both in space and in time, vouched for an effort towards modernization and adjustment to the changing outlook of the age.

The cult of plastic values at the beginning of the century was followed by that quest of expression, of movement and the evolution of forms which was carried to almost startling lengths by the last great painter of the School of Seville, Juan de Valdés Leal. In his passionate art the restraint and sure taste of Murillo are far to seek ; it is full of dramatic *trouvailles*, bold surprises. In Leal's uneven, sometimes over-hasty execution, color reigns supreme. The artist draws directly with his brush, and excels in rendering scenes of violence, falling bodies, hurried movements. There are amazing anticipations of the art of a much later date in some of his procedures in the field of color, though these are probably more empirical and instinctive than consciously contrived—notably in his juxtapositions of bright patches making the picture surface throb with light and life. In the composition, left partly empty, of his *Vanities* (in the Hospital of La Caridad, Seville) the foreshortenings in the foreground are highly effective, notably as regards the head of the dead knight of St James, which evokes Goya's most dramatic etchings.

BARTOLOMÉ ESTEBAN MURILLO (1618-1682). THE IMMACULATE CONCEPTION (SO-CALLED
SAN ILDEFONSO VERSION). DETAIL. PRADO, MADRID.

THE WORLD OF VELAZQUEZ

★

THE SCHOOL OF MADRID

THE SPANISH PAINTERS OF THE

EIGHTEENTH CENTURY

DIEGO VELAZQUEZ (1599-1660). PORTRAIT OF PHILIP IV, CA. 1628. (79½ × 40½″)
PRADO, MADRID.

THE WORLD OF VELAZQUEZ

AFTER the close of the Renaissance painters were called on to solve a twofold problem at once psychological and technical. Both the question of the subject and that of its interpretation (in other words the picture surface) had now to be envisaged from a new angle. Whereas the Primitives had been able to build up and enliven their compositions by inserting details which were equally effective whether interconnected or treated as independent units, the new, rationalistic outlook on the world called for a synthetic integration of the picture in terms of a single dominant idea, clearly stated and stripped of all accessories ; likewise of a set, fully planned compositional lay-out. Henceforth the subject reigned supreme, served by a deliberately impersonal technique lending itself equally well to any kind of representation. Caravaggio, who was the outstanding figure of the reaction against the frigid academicism which inevitably set in, solved the problem by focusing shafts of vivid light on the leading elements of the subject (on faces, for example) and also by emphasizing gestures. But in so doing he had to sacrifice the rest of the picture; thus backgrounds and garments became inert, amorphous masses of obscurity. The Spanish painters cast about for remedies for this erosion of the picture surface by encroaching shadows, vast tracts of all-devouring gloom—though in its way this seeming will to self-annihilation suited the Spanish temperament. Towards the end of his life Ribera brightened his palette and tried to impart to daylight scenes the vivid sheen and effects of strong relief produced by artificial light or cross-lighting. And there was enough of the Primitive in Zurbaran's artistic personality to lead him to diversify his compositions— often to the happiest effect—with unexpected details, still lifes and architectural passages.

In his early days Velazquez kept more or less to Zurbaran's methods. His Seville pictures have a curious intricacy ; themes are developed on several planes, the leading theme being sometimes relegated to the back of the composition and placed in an opening or window under the stronger light pouring in from the back of the scene ; an example is *Christ in the House of Martha* (National Gallery, London). There is no question here as in some works of this century, Poussin's for instance, of integrating the human element in some vast landscape setting into which it merges naturally and appropriately ; we find, rather, what is nothing short of an invasion of the picture by a crowd of incidental figures, objects and still lifes, which, treated as separate units, acquire a disproportionate value and significance. Sometimes indeed the differences of scale are such that the effect is one of real clumsiness ; still we must not forget that Velazquez was very young when he painted these pictures. The elements do not hold together and even seem incongruous ; nor can we assume, as we certainly can in the case of Zurbaran's mature work, that these anomalies are deliberate or instinctive, or that the painter is seeking to interpret the mysterious rhythms and consonances of the universe by bringing together apparently ill-assorted objects. No, all that these early works prove is that Velazquez in his youth was well aware of the danger threatening the painting of the period, that of impersonality, and, eager to avoid this, gave individual significance and a precise value to each of the persons or objects in his composition. In his first phase such considerations took precedence of that overall conception of the picture which in his later work was to predominate so strongly and so brilliantly. Indeed no other painter shows us a world so coherent and so homogeneous, yet so varied, as that of Velazquez after his arrival in Madrid. Meanwhile one thing he learnt from these early ventures was an amazing intensity of observation of his models and a habit of attaching individual importance to each of their features.

It is this that in the past led some to regard Velazquez as an amazing ' eye,' functioning mechanically like a camera lens, and as little more. We today realize how short-sighted was this view, not less so than the view of those who saw in his most famous works mere ' slices of life,' and contrasting these with the erudite, abstract compositions of the Roman school, regarded Velazquez as sponsoring a return to concrete everyday reality. The picture usually cited in support of this view is *The Spinners* which, we are told, was the outcome of a visit which Velazquez made, accompanied by some ladies of the Court, to the Santa Isabel tapestry-factory. But such theories are now seen to be due to a misconception of

DIEGO VELAZQUEZ (1599-1660). DON BALTASAR CARLOS ON HORSEBACK, CA. 1634. (82×68″)
PRADO, MADRID.

DIEGO VELAZQUEZ (1599-1660). THE SURRENDER OF BREDA, 1634-1635. (120¾ × 144¼″)
PRADO, MADRID.

the facts ; since the publication of a scholarly and convincing description by Diego Angulo Iñiguez of the manner in which Velazquez built up his major works, there can be no further doubt as to the true sources of his art and the basic elements of his compositions.

The fact that reminiscences of classical figures were to be found in Velazquez' work —for example of Michelangelo's *Pensieroso* in his *Mars*—had already been observed. Attention had also been drawn to his handling of mythological scenes and his way of bringing down the gods of Olympus to the human level, to the point of making them ridiculous; indeed Ortega y Gasset went so far as to declare that " Velazquez used his brush as a broom to sweep away the gods." By a close study of Velazquez' masterworks Diego Angulo has revealed the latent presence in them of certain pre-existing forms which, however, are combined, interpreted and transfigured with a skill that is little short of magical. There is nothing derogatory to the artist in such research ; on the contrary, by indicating the treasures of the past on which Velazquez drew, it shows how, behind his amazing naturalness and simplicity, lay the workings of a prodigiously alert mind, a vast store of knowledge and, above all, that mysterious alchemy which is an apanage of the great artist. Far from recording camera-wise his first visual impression, Velazquez thinks out his composition, bearing in mind the store of ' referents ' he has accumulated from his days in Pacheco's studio onward, by the study of engravings, the pictures in the royal collections (especially those by the artists he most admired, such as El Greco and Veronese), and those which he saw in the course of his travels at the most famous art centers of Spain and Italy and especially in the Sistine Chapel. Thus when he was to paint a picture he began by conjuring up in his mind's eye appropriate rhythms or happy arrangements of details which had struck him in these 'referents' and often used them as his starting-off point.

Diego Angulo's analysis of *Las Lanzas* (better known as *The Surrender of Breda*) is a case in point. Velazquez was required to paint for the Sala de los Reinos in the new palace, Buen Retiro, in which scenes of the great Spanish victories were hung, a picture commemorating the surrender of Breda, the Dutch fortified town which after a long siege had capitulated to the Spanish commander, Spinola. In recognition of the heroic defense of the town Spinola accorded to the Dutch commander, Justin of Nassau, all the honors of war, and it was this chivalrous encounter between the victor and the vanquished, a moment when the sense of fellowship between brave men prevailed over the savagery of warfare, rather than a scene of battle, that Velazquez chose for his theme. It is obvious that even though he may have obtained descriptions of the incident from eyewitnesses, the painter had to go beyond these if he was to sublimate a particular occasion, dramatic though it was, into one of a more general, loftier import. What he did was to create a picture that is a wholly original synthesis of invented elements—or, more accurately, elements borrowed from other representations, on which, however, he everywhere imposes his personal imprint. The result, in any case, was one of the finest pictures that exists, one of those supreme works in which everything seems inevitable, as if it could not have been otherwise.

As had already been observed by Paul Jamot, the general lay-out of *Las Lanzas* was taken from one of Bernard Salomon's illustrations to the *Quatrains historiques de la Bible* by Canon Claude Paradin (published in 1553 at Lyons), which depicts the meeting of Abraham and Melchisedec. The resemblances with this engraving are too striking to be ascribed to chance. It shows Melchisedec in a humble attitude offering bread to Abraham, who is at the head of a troop of warriors carrying long pikes. Not only is the general arrangement of the two groups the same as that of the Dutch and the Spaniards in Velazquez' picture, but Abraham, who wears a cuirass, is extending his arm with the same gesture as Spinola's, while a regiment marches past behind, just as in *Las Lanzas*. True, the execution is completely different in the two works, but this was only to be expected, considering that Salomon's is only a rather perfunctorily made book illustration, while *Las Lanzas* is one of the largest pictures known to art. Starting from this premise, Velazquez drew inspiration from two infinitely greater masters, El Greco and Veronese: from the *Espolio* and *The Centurion praying Christ to heal his palsied Son*, to be precise. The last-named work, now in the Prado, is said to have been acquired by Philip IV when the collection of King Charles I of England was dispersed, in 1649. This means either that Velazquez had seen it previously, perhaps during his visit to Italy, or else, as is not impossible, that *Las Lanzas* was painted considerably later than 1635, the date hitherto assigned to it. For it is impossible to doubt that in painting *Las Lanzas* Velazquez had in mind the slow, majestic movement and the warm, rich colorscheme of *The Centurion*. Moreover Spinola in *Las Lanzas* employs the same gesture as the centurion stretching out his arms towards Christ, while the group attending Justin has the same arrangement as that of the group of apostles. Particularly noteworthy is the bright white patch made by the coat of the soldier who is pointing with his finger, and the dark profile of another soldier telling out against it; in the Italian picture Christ's breast is similarly illuminated and on its left we see the profile of a Negro. As for the group of Spaniards, Velazquez obviously had El Greco in mind; indeed he never made a secret of what he owed to that master, whom he revered and some of whose pictures he is known to have possessed. The almost amorphous mass of figures composing Abraham's bodyguard in the Salomon print is here replaced by an animated, skillfully ordered assemblage of faces shown at various angles ranging from side- to full-face, in a medley of scarves and armor recalling the famous picture in the Cathedral of Toledo. The nudes in *Vulcan's Forge* and *Joseph's Coat* (painted before this, in 1630) are generally held to be reminiscences of Velazquez'

DIEGO VELAZQUEZ (1599-1660). DON BALTASAR CARLOS IN HUNTING COSTUME, 1635-1636. DETAIL.
PRADO, MADRID.

DIEGO VELAZQUEZ (1599-1660). STAG'S HEAD, CA. 1636. (26 × 20 ½")
COLLECTION OF THE MARQUIS OF CASA TORRES, MADRID.

first stay in Italy and his encounters with classical Italian art. Actually, however, the central figure in the *Forge*, seen from behind, exactly reproduces the attitude and the strong muscular development of the Saint's companion in the *Saint Maurice* at the Escorial. Similarly the half-naked man sheltering himself with his arm whom we see on the left is exactly paralleled in El Greco's *Christ driving the Traders from the Temple* and *Healing of the Blind Man*.

Thus here we have further proof of the great influence of El Greco in Spain during the whole first half of the XVIIth century. Indeed his *œuvre* was a mine of discoveries for the artists, and Velazquez in particular learnt much not only from the bold innovations and foreshortenings of El Greco's composition, but also from his method of dappling uniform backgrounds with flakes of color and hatchings, bringing out the living, vibrating quality of light. El Greco's impact on Spanish art was greater than that of Dürer which, profound and lasting though it, too, was, took effect by way of black-and-white prints and was thus confined to draftsmanship and composition. In *Joseph's Coat* the general lay-out and particularly the figure of Jacob and even the curious expression of his face stem directly from that of the high priest in the engraving of *Jesus before Caiaphas*.

But Diego Angulo's most remarkable discovery relates to *The Spinners*. One of the painter's last works, this was long regarded as a sort of excursion on his part into naturalism, a fragment of visual experience rendered from the life. Actually it is ordered throughout by a fixed compositional lay-out deriving from Michelangelo's ceiling at the Sistine Chapel. Mengs showed better understanding than modern art-historians when he wrote: " This picture is made in such a way that we feel the hand played no part in its execution, but the artist's will alone." The two women spinning wool in the foreground, on whom the whole composition hinges, one seen full face with her leg stretched forward, the other slewed round in a sinuous movement, with her leg bent and an arm extended, reproduce the attitudes of two of the four symbolical figures seated on blocks of stone in front of Michelangelo's central panel, in which God is seen creating the world. The proportions of this panel are the same as those of the background scene of *The Spinners*, in which we see, above a sort of stage, the brilliantly lit tapestry depicting the myth of Arachne who was changed by Minerva into a spider as a punishment for having woven a representation of Jupiter's *amours* and the Rape of Europa. It certainly required no little courage thus to adapt the Sistine decoration, revered no less for its associations with the almost superhuman genius of Michelangelo than for the sacred nature of its theme, to a representation of women, obviously peasant types, spinning wool in a modern workroom. But in these reminiscences is neither pedantry nor disrespect: they tell of the deep impression Michelangelo had made on Velazquez, and of this alone. (It is, perhaps, significant that in the inventory made of his library after his death, besides many books dealing with anatomy and sculpture, and even magic, were two on Michelangelo's painting and sculpture.) Nor must we overlook Raphael's influence, plain to see in such pictures as *Vulcan's Forge*. Pacheco tells us that during his first visit to Italy Velazquez applied himself to studying humbly and conscientiously not only the masterpieces to be seen at Rome but the great Venetians as well. Cardinal Barberini's patronage opened to him the doors of the Vatican: thus he could feast his eyes at leisure on Raphael's and Michelangelo's frescos and he made pencil drawings of them, filled out with color. It was natural that his prolonged contacts with the art of the Italian Renaissance —Velazquez' first stay in Italy lasted some eighteen months and he visited Ferrara, Bologna, Florence and Naples—served to confirm the feeling he had had from the start that only the respect of ideal or geometrical proportions can give that " solid and durable " quality distinctive of all great art to evocations of fleeting, everyday reality.

While it is true that the world of Velazquez differs from that of the Renaissance with its emphasis on formal archetypes, we must not forget that he stands for a new idealism, far more than for any instinctual ' return to nature.' The difference is that his method of approach enables him to take over *all* that life has to offer. His predecessors had sought to find in nature forms approximating to their ideal of perfectly balanced proportions, and in pursuit of this ideal did not hesitate to do violence to reality and strip it of much that was most

DIEGO VELAZQUEZ (1599-1660). PHILIP IV HUNTING THE WILD BOAR, 1636 OR 1638. (74×123″)
NATIONAL GALLERY, LONDON.
REPRODUCED BY COURTESY OF THE TRUSTEES

vital in it. Velazquez' procedure was exactly the contrary of theirs. His starting-point was a synthesis or schema deriving from his profound awareness of geometrical proportions and pictorial rhythms, this schema being so vividly present in his mind as to have for him almost a concrete existence, and into it he fitted all the forms of life itself without distinction. Thus his visual experience ended up—if by way of slow and gradual approximations—by strictly conforming with the pattern he had in his mind. We need only observe how patiently Velazquez worked, how unremitting was his quest of perfection: how after several years' interval he would correct the position of a leg, an arm, the crease in a garment. Each of his *pentimenti* brings him nearer to the perfection he glimpsed on his first visual contact with the subject. This is as true of his portraits (often wrongly regarded as more ' spontaneous ') as of his large compositions. Velazquez never improvises, never surrenders to instinct or takes short cuts. Always he ponders, thinks things out. Owing to chemical changes in the pigment which cause light passages to become transparent after a certain time, the retouchings can now be seen: they reveal the successive stages by which he built up his pictures, and strangely enough, give an impression of a certain preliminary restlessness lurking beneath the impassibility achieved in the finished work. Considering the infinite pains Velazquez lavished on each of his canvases, we need not be surprised by the relative smallness of his output. Of the several hundred works which used to be attributed to him, Aureliano de Beruete, for technical reasons, eliminated all but ninety-five. Since then, however, further research by Allende-Salazar has brought this figure up to the neighborhood of a hundred and twenty. Even allowing for some sixty pictures that have disappeared, the total may seem small for the life's work of a painter who devoted himself heart and soul to his art.

When Velazquez created the modern landscape, this was not due to his sudden discovery of the beauty of any specific scene of nature ; it would be truer to say that he consciously applied himself to a re-interpretation of the work of his predecessors, especially the Flemish landscapists. Already in his Seville days he had made a rather clumsy move in this direction when he employed a background of leafage in his austere portrait of Cristobal Suarez de

56

Ribera. Ten years later (passing no doubt through intermediate stages of which no trace survives) Velazquez had completely mastered the art of the landscape, as is evident in the portraits of Olivares and the Infante Baltasar Carlos on horseback, and subsequently in those of the King and princes in hunting dress: in all of which landscape plays a prominent part. This was not due to mere chance: the artist knew very well what he was about when he posed his models against backgrounds that grew steadily brighter in hue, with the result that faces and details of clothing told out more strongly against them. But there was more to it than this: those open-air settings enabled the artist not only to give a fuller and subtler sense of depth, but also to impart to the entire picture surface the rhythms implicit in the figures. For it is obvious in these pictures that the landscape is not intended to represent any specific scene, but conditioned by the posture of the figure. Usually Velazquez employs much the same lay-out: the model is posed on the side of a hill, with the result that the ground slopes away, fringed by small trees shaken by the wind that dwindle out into the distance. Half way up the canvas we see an undulating, more sharply defined line, the summit of a mountain-range bathed in bluish haze. Sometimes this effect of deep perspective is strengthened by a tree in the foreground against which the subject of the portrait leans. Though the same motifs recur again and again and stereotyped as are the poses, the elaborate accoutrements, and the prancing horses, each of these pictures gives an impression of complete naturalness, indeed inevitableness. The landscapes are probably no less ' arranged ' and it would be idle to seek in them any allusion to a given place, yet they evoke to perfection the countryside around Madrid, with its vast, almost bare horizon, and the color of the distant Sierras. This atmosphere and the same horizon are present even in *Las Lanzas*. The landscape in a later work, *St Anthony Abbot and St Paul the Hermit*, consists of a scene in the high

DIEGO VELAZQUEZ (1599-1660) AND J. B. DEL MAZO (?-1667). VIEW OF SARAGOSSA, 1647. DETAIL. PRADO, MADRID.

DIEGO VELAZQUEZ (1599-1660). THE BUFFOON DON SEBASTIAN DE MORA, CA. 1648. (41¾×32″)
PRADO, MADRID.

mountains cleft by a vast gap, and Diego Angulo has pointed out that while the composition is inspired by Dürer, there are passages taken over almost line for line from Patinir's landscapes. Some of this painter's finest works, now amongst the most treasured possessions of the Prado, were already in the royal collection, which included a hunting scene by Cranach.

Velazquez painted several pictures of Philip IV out hunting. Only one of these is extant, *The Boar Hunt* (also known as *Philip IV hunting the Wild Boar*) in the National Gallery, London, and it is perhaps the finest example of the genre. Here the landscape is treated frankly as the leading theme, though there is an animated, skillfully handled central scene and a crowded foreground. So as to give a clear view of the enclosure in which the hunt is taking place, the painter has employed a bird's-eye perspective, the effect of which is that the background is rendered on the same scale as the foreground. In the arena-like lists we see tiny horsemen galloping armed with long white staves, their silhouettes delicately blurred, while in front we see ranged along the barriers a motley crowd of fully a hundred people, a sort of muster of all Velazquez' figures: grandees in gay attire, men dressed in black, peasants with their horses or donkeys, dogs held in leash by attendants, children, men drinking, beggars in brown cloaks. A recent, very thorough cleaning has brought out the boldness and brilliancy of the colors: the carriages in which the Queen and her suite are following the hunt are bright blue, while the patches of red, yellow and sky-blue of the men's garments, the greys and a varied range of browns combine in skillful modulations. The attitudes, equally diversified, come out quite clearly despite the small size of the figures. But vivacious as is the rendering of the 'hunt,' most fascinating of all is the landscape in the background, a stretch of rolling country treated as a continuous whole and wonderfully harmonious in effect with its long smooth tree-clad slopes interspersed with bright patches of sandy soil. Here the landscape has not a secondary role, as in the portraits: for the first time it exists in its own right, as a living presence: indeed the central scene is so arranged as to accord with it. If that scene is removed (as can easily be done by screening the lower part of the picture), we have a superb rendering of a natural scene as full of life as any of Constable's or Courbet's, and realized on a vaster scale, in deeper recession. I hardly think the small views of the Gardens of the Villa Medici are up to the level of the hunting scene, great as is their reputation. In these sketches, which undoubtedly were made on the spot, we have as it were a foretaste of the XVIIIth-century fondness for ruins and time-scarred monuments: but the trim, well-ordered Medici gardens are a far cry indeed from the magnificent synthetic rendering of wild nature in the hunting scene.

Velazquez often called in his assistant Juan Bautista del Mazo, who married his daughter, to help him, especially in his backgrounds and landscapes. Mazo shows agreeably poetic feeling but lacks vigor and precision: his landscapes are relatively feeble, lusterless reflections of those by Velazquez. The order for the *View of Saragossa*, painted to commemorate the visit to that city made by the King and Baltasar Carlos, some months before the young prince's death, was given to Mazo. In this case it was Velazquez who acted as collaborator and we can see how important was his contribution, notably in the clean-cut, sinuous contours of the buildings and the little specks of color indicating, with the delicate precision of a Guardi or a Corot, figures which are reflected in the greenish water.

It was now that he invented what Rafael Benet in his interesting observations on Velazquez' "Platonism" names "chromatic form," to implement that marvellous fusion between the ideal and the real which he now was by way of achieving. Little by little he came to steep the subject in convergent lights, whose effect was to make it, too, a source of illumination; this is the case with some of the faces, which acquire modeling and relief not by contrasts of light and shade but by a superimposition of colored planes. He used this technique to wonderful effect in dealing with elaborate embroidery and glossy silks, which at once absorb light and emit it. Thus these forms reduplicate themselves, as it were, in color vibrations perceptible beyond their surfaces. We have the most striking example of this procedure in *Las Meninas (The Maids of Honor)*, the climax of that great trilogy which includes *The Surrender of Breda* and *The Spinners*.

In this picture something happens, which had not happened in any picture before it; it is as though the canvas ceased to be an obstacle, a surface, and the spectator himself is drawn into the picture. One might even go further and say the picture comes forward to invite him in. I can recall no other work of art that produces quite this effect except Rembrandt's *Night Watch*, painted twelve years previously. The strange thing is that we seem to step into both these pictures so easily and so naturally, though each of them is a closed world and quite unfamiliar to us. Painted in 1656, *Las Meninas* was originally named *The Family*; the name under which it has become world-famous was given it for the first time in the Prado Catalog of 1843. The composition is concentric, with the little Infanta Margarita Maria as its focal point; the other figures gravitate around her like planets of an intricate, subtly ordered system, and reflect her light. The nearest, the first to catch the rays—and it is fitting that the picture's title should indicate their importance—are the two Maids of Honor: Doña Maria Agustina Sarmiento kneeling on the left, and on the right, slightly in retreat and in the middle of a curtsy, Doña Isabel de Velasco. The figure of Velazquez standing at his canvas on the extreme left rather abruptly closes the hemicycle, which ends less emphatically on the right, with two dimly lit figures, the duenna Doña Marcela de Ulloa and an unidentified man. Another winding stream of light takes its rise towards the right, where the Infanta's figure is balanced, beyond the plump, misshapen female dwarf Mari-Barbola and the sleepy mastiff lying in the foreground, by the charming little dwarf Nicolasilo Portusato.

The distribution of the various elements, not to mention the exquisite rendering of the details, is certainly one of the most expert known to art. For one thing we may note the dexterous arrangement of the verticals: that of the stretcher to the huge canvas on which Velazquez is working pointing at a slight angle towards the ceiling, while on the right the little dwarf's leg resting on the dog's back (this is a *pentimento*, the leg was originally straight) makes a diagonal in the opposite direction. The result is that despite the light coming from a window on the right, the picture as a whole seems to draw on a source of light located well in front, on the left. And a third light builds up as it were a luminous pyramid whose apex lies between the Infanta and Doña Isabel de Velasco: the patch of daylight in the doorway at the back, giving on a flight of steps, on which stands Don José Nieto Velazquez (Master of the Queen's tapestry and doubtless a relative of the painter), a tall black figure on a white ground in the act of turning to contemplate the scene in the room. Full of interest, too, is the artist's handling of this passage: contrasted with the man's supple, natural movement we have the rigid structure of the open door, deliberately emphasized by the entering light—an almost abstract pattern of alternating squares and rectangles. A mirror on the wall beside the door reflects the faces of the King and Queen, who obviously could not be left out, and are thus discreetly given the place of honor; their dignity forbidding their appearance in the flesh in the miscellaneous group of lively figures in the foreground. The wall hung with copies made by Mazo after Rubens, the ceiling with its dark fixtures for the hanging chandeliers and the side-wall with closed windows—all combine to make an austere architectural setting, whose severity, however, is softened by the play of shadows: just the setting needed to bring out the aerial, flower-like grace of Velazquez' painting, the pale gold of the Infanta's hair, the creamy whites of her dress, the soft pinks and yellows of the ribbons, and to enhance the silvery beauty of the light flooding the whole tall room.

Here so well devised and thought-out is the composition that we can hardly credit the generally accepted story: that Velazquez was painting the King and Queen when, unexpectedly, the little princess came in with her attendants and the painter broke off the work he was engaged on so as to record the impression made by their charming group. To mention only one point, the size of the canvas in front of him seems too large for even an official portrait (though it might quite well be that of the *Meninas*). If we must have an explanation it is probably to be found in Velazquez' self-portrait. When this man, naturally so modest, thus depicted himself, with dignity it is true, but with the tools so to speak of his trade, brush and palette, in his hand, was it not his intention to present the monarch who had

DIEGO VELAZQUEZ (1599-1660). LAS MENINAS, 1656. (125 × 108½″)
PRADO, MADRID.

showed him such unvarying kindness, friendship and understanding, with a token of his respect and affection ? And was not the presence of a man we may assume to have been a relative intended to suggest the devotion of his family as a whole ? With loving care he grouped in front of him the persons it was his function to paint, with special emphasis on the little princess Margarita, the first-born of Philip's second marriage, the child on whom his

DIEGO VELAZQUEZ (1599-1660). LAS MENINAS, 1656. DETAIL: THE INFANTA MARGARITA.
PRADO, MADRID.

DIEGO VELAZQUEZ (1599-1660). LAS MENINAS, 1656. DETAIL: DON JOSÉ NIETO VELAZQUEZ
AND DOÑA ISABEL DE VELASCO. PRADO, MADRID.

DIEGO VELAZQUEZ (1599-1660). LAS MENINAS, 1656. DETAIL : SELF-PORTRAIT OF VELAZQUEZ.
PRADO, MADRID.

hopes were centered in the dark period through which Spain and the Spanish monarchy were passing. It may not have been mere chance that the scene was located in one of the rooms which had been occupied by poor little Baltasar Carlos, doomed to an early death, and is there not a significant parallelism between the many portraits of the boy prince on whom so many hopes were centered, painted by Velazquez twenty years before, and those of the Infanta Margarita which are now the glory of the Prado, the Louvre, the Museum of Vienna and the Duke of Alba's collection ? Sanchez Canton draws attention to the fact that the Infanta Maria Teresa, Philip's daughter by his first wife, does not appear in the picture and suggests that this was because she was severely criticizing the policy her father was following at this time. Here the faithful artist offers to his sovereign his masterpiece, the summing-up of his life's work and the finest flower of the skill he has attained, sparing no pains to make this homage, testament of an artist who lived for his art, pleasing to his royal patron. Nor did the King fail to realize this; he hung the picture in his bedroom and later, after Velazquez' death, had the Red Cross of the Order of Santiago (awarded him shortly before his death) painted on the artist's breast.

With its melancholy, benevolent gaze, this self-portrait has more to tell us than any other about Velazquez' appearance and personality. A work of the artist's youth, now in the Prado (dated 1623), thought by some to be a self-portrait and showing us a man with black, brooding eyes, broad nostrils and fleshy lips, hints at a sensual temperament kept under stern control. But perhaps this is the painter's brother. Suggestions have also been made that some figures in his compositions are likenesses of himself: for instance the kneeling man with a gipsy-like face in *The Adoration of the Magi* (some have even wondered if Velazquez had not some African blood in his veins); also the Spanish soldier with a plumed hat on the right of the horse in *Las Lanzas*. There is a self-portrait in the Pinacoteca Capitolina in Rome, supposed to have been made in Italy in 1630 ; it shows a man with a bushy shock of hair and a far-away, nonchalant gaze. At Munich and Florence, too, are alleged self-portraits, but these are so dissimilar that Allende-Salazar regards as authentic—apart from that in *Las Meninas*—only the self-portrait (ca. 1638-1640) in the Museum of Valencia, which shows Velazquez as an already aging man, looking rather prim in his starched collar and gazing vaguely into the distance. Though he was fifty-six when he painted it, his portrait in *Las Meninas* shows a man with unimpaired intellectual powers and keen lucidity, whose pondering gaze bears out Palomino's dictum: " When the eye sees, it is thinking."

This marks the culminating point of the painter's brilliant career. At this last stage of a crowded life, the passing years have lost their hold on him, he is merged, heart and soul, into the work that is to give him immortality. How much ground had been covered since the days when thirty-seven years earlier the young Sevillian, whose drawing was so firm and accurate and who showed such skill in conjuring strongly plastic forms out of masses of darkness plunged in dazzling light, had made his first attempt upon the Court of Madrid ! Enraptured by the vigor of his first portraits, the young king had taken to the painter at once and it was the beginning of a lifelong friendship. To this Velazquez responded by adapting himself whole-heartedly to the life of the perfect courtier, a life of tactful deference, involving many sacrifices and total loyalty. Indeed, his painting, like his life, was one long service of his monarch. Henceforth the Palace was his home, and he combined with his duties as Court Painter the brilliant, if exacting career of a Palace official, being successively Gentleman Usher, Officer of the Royal Wardrobe, Inspector of Works in the Palace and, from 1652 till his death, Grand Marshal of the Palace. With Mayno he supervised the installation of the new Buen Retiro Palace; he was deputed by the King to select and buy works of art, and the Spanish royal collections, then the best in Europe, owed much to his sure taste and wise counsels. The purpose of his second journey to Italy was the purchase of works by the Venetians, Ribera and others. The catalog of the Alcazar, compiled in 1686, lists no less than six hundred and fourteen pictures by the greatest masters. As Grand Marshal of the Palace, Velazquez was responsible for the arrangements of the King's journeys and festivals. He organized those grandiose ceremonies, gay or somber, which

DIEGO VELAZQUEZ (1599-1660). QUEEN MARIANA OF AUSTRIA, CA. 1653. DETAIL.
PRADO, MADRID.

marked the course of Philip's reign: for example, the completion of the crypt at the Escorial, burial place of the Spanish Kings, the meeting in the Isle of Pheasants (in the Bidassoa) in connection with the marriage of the Infanta Maria Teresa to King Louis XIV. On this occasion all the decorations and pageantry, both of the utmost magnificence, though guided by a sober not to say austere good taste, were placed in Velazquez' hands, and when he returned to the capital at the end of June 1660 he was thoroughly worn out. Indeed the strain had been too much for him and on August 6 he died, deeply mourned by his royal master.

From 1623 onwards his whole life's work had been bound up with the life of the Court. Almost effortlessly he had abandoned the easy-going world of his southern youth, with its picturesque local color and accessibility to foreign influences, and found his footing in that strange, shut-in world of the Spanish Court, where the most punctilious, intricate etiquette known to Europe was the order of the day and into which no sounds or rumors of the outside world were permitted to intrude. Yet it was not so far estranged from reality as might seem at first sight; were not dwarfs and buffoons, whose high-sounding names were parodies of the nobility, to be seen in the very shadow of the throne, grotesque reminders of the ultimate futility of all human pomp and pride? Again and again Velazquez painted his king, and in the long succession of portraits, some official, some more intimate, even indeed in the formal poses, we can trace year by year the changes that came over Philip, his inexorable progress from a slender, shy, idealistic youth to a thickset, heavy-jowled man, who has suffered deeply and is crushed under the load of his responsibilities. Yet the features hardly change. How well Velazquez understood this man with the sad, gentle eyes and

DIEGO VELAZQUEZ (1599-1660). THE INFANTA MARGARITA MARIA, 1659-1660. DETAIL.
PRADO, MADRID.

sensual lips, who, if an indifferent sovereign, weak-willed and conscious of his weakness, was nevertheless large-hearted, a true friend of the arts, a kindly, understanding, very human man, whose long reign, if it brought little good to his country, was a golden age for Castilian art and literature. He alone seemed permanent in this Court where all seemed doomed to premature decay, where the young people, victims of a congenital disease, with their specter-pale faces and unhealthily flushed cheeks, went one by one to early graves, but not before the king of painters had given them vicarious immortality. How lightly, delicately, Velazquez traces the features of these phantom figures: the King's brothers, the Cardinal Infante Ferdinand with his long, sad face, Don Carlos, a drab replica of the King himself; his pretty sister Maria who had won the heart of Charles I of England before marrying the Emperor; the King's first wife Isabelle de Bourbon, daughter of Henry IV, a strong-willed, full-blooded woman who could not endure the stifling atmosphere of the Court and was constantly involved in love-affairs. She was the only one of them who disliked sitting for Velazquez, whom she suspected of being a tool of her *bête-noire*, Olivares. But it was for the royal children that Velazquez reserved his tenderest accents; no brushstrokes could be gayer, subtler, tenderer, than those he lavishes on the little prince Baltasar Carlos who charms us still with his candid, thoughtful face and the natural dignity of his bearing.

But soon all alike had vanished from the scene; King Philip alone lived on into the dark days of Spain's decline. He married his young niece, formerly betrothed to Baltasar Carlos, and started a new family. Velazquez has given us pictures of the girl queen in all her youthful health and beauty, but the Spanish Court seemed to be under a curse; she too was destined all too soon to languish in its stifling atmosphere of routine and *ennui*. At twenty years' interval he painted portrait after portrait of the little Infanta Margarita Maria in whom the childish grace of Baltasar Carlos seemed to have come to life again. Altogether he made seven portraits of her at different ages, but unlike her half brother she seemed to develop very little; her face remained as insipid as her life, ruined by an ill-assorted marriage. But in painting her lustrous dresses with those gigantic, heavily embroidered panier skirts which seem so strange to modern eyes, Velazquez found scope for his most luminous brush-strokes and happiest effects.

Meanwhile like a sort of counterpoint to the royal theme there came the series of pictures of freaks and half-wits: from the Court buffoon Pablo de Valladolid, standing like an actor with his chest puffed out, an absurd black form against a featureless yellow background—this was the picture which so much impressed Manet when he visited the Prado in 1865, a year before painting *The Fifer*—to those unhappy children, a counterpoise to the young princes, such as the hydrocephalous idiot boy of Vallecas, who was the Infante's 'personal' dwarf. Others, such as the dwarf El Primo poring over enormous tomes, are caricatures of philosophers, or of great generals, like the poor creature ironically known as " Don John of Austria." Strangest of all, perhaps, are those who have no particularly ugly traits, for instance the dwarf Don Sebastian de Mora, whose look is frankly tragic, or that little creature misnamed " El Inglés " who faces us so proudly, his puny stature redeemed by the sheer gorgeousness of his costume, all in brown and gold. And, lastly, there are those queer little beings in *Las Meninas*... To all his models alike Velazquez imparts a truly human quality; even when their features are set and prim, or ravaged by the years, he makes us feel the dignity of man's estate. He paints without the least *parti pris*; perhaps indeed the very restrictions of his official life encouraged in him, paradoxically enough, that superb detachment and total unconstraint in his art. Under his brush anomalies disappear. That technique which had been the wonder of Rubens and the Italians advanced, without a break, from strength to strength; familiar forms assume new aspects, evoke new resonances, while the colors acquire a new significance, new luster. He was not a one-track painter, yet he seems to choose for each figure hues that are peculiarly his. He had all the colors known to art at his command, but under his brush there was always some special quality, eluding definition, about them; perhaps they were what in Perrault's fairy tale are naïvely thought to be invisible: *couleurs du temps*.

DIEGO VELAZQUEZ (1599-1660). THE SPINNERS, CA. 1657. DETAIL : THE LEGEND OF ARACHNE.
PRADO, MADRID.

THE SCHOOL OF MADRID

Combining as he so brilliantly did the functions of a high Court functionary and of King's Painter, Velazquez had achieved a status far above that of any other painter of his age. Yet, vast as was his prestige, his personal influence and that of his art took effect only on those closely associated with him, in other words his assistants: his son-in-law Juan Bautista del Mazo and his slave Juan de Pareja who remained devoted to his ex-master after his emancipation—both, as it so happened, indifferent painters. Only men of Velazquez' own caliber could have understood his message. Generations had to pass before first Goya, then Manet, studied his technique so eagerly and to such effect, and they, in fact, were his true successors. (In much the same way he himself had studied El Greco and the Masters of the past.) Meanwhile he had bequeathed to Spain types of the Court portrait which were to persist for several decades and were imitated by the painters of the next king, Carreño de Miranda and Coello. Nevertheless their talents had been shaped differently; there was never in any effective sense a " School of Velazquez."

On the other hand a School of Madrid, with distinctive characteristics, manifested in a series of large-scale religious decorations, flourished from the end of the XVIth century onwards. The city had grown greatly since the monarchs of the House of Austria had made it their capital, and a host of artists had come to work at the Buen Retiro, the Alcazar and neighboring palaces. Moreover the wealthy religious communities kept the artists busy; a large number of churches and convents date from the XVIIth century. Thus there was a great demand for frescos, and in painting them the Spanish artists imitated the Italian painters bidden by the King to the Escorial.

Little studied as yet, this school began as a provincial movement; its earliest leaders, mere names to us today—men like Pedro de las Cuevas, under whom studied Carreño, Francisco Rizi and Pereda—were merely expert craftsmen who taught the arts of the portrait and the still life. Meanwhile the Court painters, who were of Italian origin, Carducho, Caxès, Nardi (Velazquez' rivals), conducted a vigorous campaign with their works, their teaching and in the case of Carducho by the written word as well, in favor of classical composition and an impersonal style of execution enabling the artist to treat contemporary themes on the same lines as biblical or mythological subjects.

The first generation of Madrid painters included many of Cuevas' pupils: Antonio Arias Fernandez, a good, severely naturalistic draftsman, Francisco Camilo, Jusepe Leonardo who painted battle-scenes in far-flung landscape settings (the battle-piece was then in high favor, its leading exponents being a retired Army Captain Juan de Toledo and Juan de la Corte, and the creation of the *Sala de las Reinos*, ' Hall of the Kingdoms,' at the Buen Retiro was a token of its popularity), and lastly two painters who were really great artists, Fray Juan Rizi and Antonio de Pereda. The former, a contemporary of Velazquez, was the son of a Bolognese painter who came with Zuccaro to work at the Escorial. At the age of twenty-seven he became a Benedictine monk, entering the monastery of Montserrat, but seems to have gone on painting as much as before. Always eager to extend his knowledge, he studied anatomy and did sketches of the nude from the living model. He produced a number of religious works, mostly for the convents of his Order, where they are still to be seen. The cycle relating to the life of St Benedict, several scenes from which are in the Prado, depicts the ordinary life of the monks inside a monastery; very different from Zurbaran's synthetic representations, it comes much nearer the French painters' realistic renderings of everyday experience. As drawing master to the Infante Baltasar Carlos, Rizi came in contact with Velazquez, some reminiscences of whose procedures, such as the use of translucent colors and an adroit handling of light, are apparent in his work. His composition is sober and unforced, his execution free and fluent. His high abilities as a portrait-painter can be seen in his likeness of Fray Alonso de San Vitores, Bishop of Almeria (now at the Museum of Burgos). He migrated to Italy in 1662 and lived for the last twenty years of his life at the Monastery of Monte Cassino.

CLAUDIO COELLO (1642-1693). PORTRAIT OF CHARLES II. (26×22″)
PRADO, MADRID.

Antonio de Pereda was born in Valladolid, where he began his art studies; he painted many large religious compositions and battle-pieces. An accurate and painstaking draftsman, he excelled in those elaborate still lifes which are the best features of his " Vanitates," the most famous of which, known as *The Dream of Life*, is in the Academy of San Fernando. Pereda does not, like Valdés Leal, overstress the moral lesson—in this context the " vanity " of man's brief life on earth—and he handles his subject with much elegance.

Thus the characteristics of this first School of Madrid may be summed up as modesty, sincerity, a scrupulous avoidance of the meretricious. To the same group belong some minor painters who specialized (like Juan and José de Arellano) in the painting of flowers, the still life and the genre landscape; thus carrying on a professional tradition which was to last until the XVIIIth century and attain its full flowering with Melendez.

The succeeding generations of painters, however, practiced a more decorative art. A pupil of Carducho, Francisco Rizi, Juan's brother, was a prolific painter of religious subjects, developing much facility in the fresco technique. Herrera the Younger, who had spent his youth in Italy and inherited his father's vehemence, showed much inventiveness in his renderings of forms in movement, figures gyrating freely in space. But the truly outstanding personality was Carreño de Miranda, an Asturian who after being trained at Valladolid, came to Madrid and worked along with Mazo as Velazquez' assistant. Mazo, though he shows sensitivity and indeed originality in his portraits, was always overshadowed by his father-in-law. It was Carreño on whom Velazquez' mantle fell after his departure from the scene. He painted the last portraits of the old king and some years later was appointed Painter of the Palace and Court Painter during the minority of the luckless Charles II. A very fine portraitist, he vividly conjures up, in the gloomy setting of the Alcazar, the melancholy aspect of the young King, a pale, unhealthy boy dressed in black, and the time-worn face of the Queen-Mother Mariana, in her widow's weeds, with her underhung jaw whose heaviness had grown more and more pronounced with age. As compared with the art of Velazquez, Carreño's betrays an over-emphasis on peculiarities and an almost neurotic exaggeration of forms. Such human characteristics as the ladies of the Court may have had are obliterated under an excited Baroque rendering of their costumes, richly decked with embroideries and upheld by fantastically wide ' hoops.' Carreño was a master of technique and he also brought a modernistic spirit into religious painting; it was he who introduced a new type of *Immaculate Conception* very different from that popularized by Murillo. Brilliant effects of pictorial construction, curiously pagan in conception as compared with that of previous Spanish artists, and heavily charged with allegories and decorative attributes, were his forte. His disciples, Cerezo, Cabezalero and especially Antoliñez (one of Francisco Rizi's pupils), imbibed the lesson of the master with excellent results, while Escalante carried the fining-down of proportions to a pitch recalling the distortions of the French etcher Bellange.

Unfortunately all these highly gifted artists died young, before any had had time to mature and give of his best. This is why a school, seemingly so rich in promise, ended so brusquely, with the century. The death of its last master, Claudio Coello, was hardly less abrupt. Of Portuguese origin, this painter was born at Madrid in 1642 and moved in Court circles from his boyhood. A pupil of Rizi and Carreño, he was the latter's successor in the favor of King Charles II. Such was the richness of his palette and so versatile his technique that he could handle the largest compositions with consummate ease. His paintings of religious subjects follow the Baroque tendencies then dominant in Spain, but he imparts to them a fine organizational balance. His masterpiece, in the Sacristy of the Escorial, depicts the King and his Court on their knees paying homage to the *Sagrada Forma*, a Host miraculously uncorrupted after nearly three hundred years, which the Prior Francisco de los Santos, attended by a group of prelates, holds aloft for their veneration. All the figures of the persons taking part in this majestic ceremony are portraits, fully characterized and convincing, while the composition as a whole is masterly; by a skillful feat of illusionist perspective the pictured architecture seems an extension of the Sacristy itself, the upper portion being peopled with angels and allegorical figures giving a striking impression of free movement in space.

LUIS PARET (1746-1799). CHARLES III AT LUNCHEON ATTENDED BY HIS COURT. (19½×25″)
PRADO, MADRID.

THE PAINTERS OF THE EIGHTEENTH CENTURY

In 1692 Charles II decided to have the ceilings of the Escorial decorated with frescos, and summoned to Madrid the Italian Luca Giordano (of " *Fa Presto* " fame) who was not only the fastest of painters but held to be the most accomplished decorator in the Baroque style. The story goes that Claudio Coello's death was hastened by the Italian's coming; hypersensitive and jealous as he was, he regarded it as a sign that he had fallen out of favor with the King. It has often been said that this sudden irruption of Giordano's gaudy, theatrical style dealt a death-blow to Spanish art. Actually, however, such art was no novelty in Spain. For some forty years the School of Madrid had been employing similar procedures, which Herrera the Younger and Francisco Rizi had brought back with them from Italy. Far from creating a break with the past the incursion of Giordano's showy art merely resuscitated, superficially and briefly, a manner of painting that the Spanish artists had already exploited and left behind. What had actually happened was that the almost simultaneous deaths (within a mere decade) of the painters of the great generations of the beginning of the century, followed by the deaths of their pupils and epigones, had resulted in a dearth of painters—another sign, perhaps, of the general enfeeblement of Spain, affecting not only her ruling class and élite but the creative spirit of the artists, which had now set in.

There is no denying the merits of Giordano's large-scale decorations and within ten years he turned out several hundred works which contributed to generalizing in all the

73

Provinces of Spain an impersonal Baroque style. With him worked a friend of Coello, Antonio Palomino, born at Bujalance near Cordova. Palomino, too, was a skillful frescoist and made some large decorations at Valencia, Salamanca and Granada, but his chief title to fame lies in his literary work, and his *Parnaso Español Pintoresco Laureado*, published between 1715 and 1724, earned him, not unjustifiably, the title of " the Spanish Vasari."

Such was the political and moral exhaustion now prevailing in Spain that there were no vigorous reactions against the accession of the new dynasty hailing from France. All the same, coming as it did after centuries of bitter conflict between the two nations, this change had deep-seated psychological effects and for several decades the latent social disequilibrium made itself felt in art. As foreigners so often are, the Bourbons were baffled and bewildered by the pride, austerity and aloofness of the Spanish temperament, and they perpetually hankered after Versailles and the elegant life of the French Court. Reciprocally, the Spanish not only felt cut off from their past but came to regard themselves as backward, out of step with the age they lived in, and to lose confidence in themselves—and this was particularly true of the artists. Thus it is not surprising that throughout the reign of Philip V French painters were called in to work for the Court: such men as René Houasse, Jean Ranc (who hailed from Montpellier and was a pompous disciple of Rigaud) and Michel Van Loo. All these men had the *métier* at their finger-tips and excelled in the stilted, academic Court portrait, but neither their work nor their personalities left any lasting mark. However René Houasse had a son, Michel-Ange, who spent much of his youth in Spain (until 1730), and came really to understand the spirit of the Spanish people. A skillful genre painter, he drew inspiration from the colorful life of the populace of Madrid, its picnics, open-air dances and frolics in the countryside and painted a number of spirited, daintily executed pictures which he submitted to the royal tapestry-factory which had just been opened, as a side-line to the cartoons on classical themes such as Don Quixote and views of the royal castles.

During the reign of Ferdinand VI work began on a new royal palace, the 'Palace of the Orient,' which was to replace the old Alcazar burnt down (in 1734) in a disastrous fire which, starting in the rooms occupied by Ranc, led to the destruction of hundreds of pictures by the great masters and many priceless treasures. Italians were commissioned to paint in fresco the ceilings of the reception rooms, grand staircase and chapel. Thus a Venetian, Amiconi, and, later, a Neapolitan, Giaquinto, were appointed Court Painters, and these men were soon to play an important part in the founding of the Academy. This, indeed, was one of the great ideas of the century: the desirability of bringing artistic creativity, hitherto essentially personal and undisciplined, under control, on 'scientific' lines and in conformity with Reason. With this in view the Academy of San Fernando was founded in 1751 under royal patronage. Instruction was given in all branches of art and the same way of seeing and rendering their vision was rigorously enforced on artists young and old, with the result that the last flickerings of Baroque were extinguished by a frigid classicism.

This movement, whose aim was to promote a culture at once generalized and based on accurate knowledge, spread to all the provinces and even to the New World. There had been in the XVIIth century some interesting attempts to create " free academies " on the lines of the big training studios of the past. Murillo's at Seville now had a new lease of life, while the academies started by Evaristo Muñoz and the Vergara brothers preceded, at Valencia, the foundation of the official Academy of San Carlos in 1768. At Saragossa where an active art tradition flourished, sponsored by Pernicharo (a pupil of Houasse), Rabiella and José Luzan, the Academy of San Luis was founded somewhat later, in 1792. Schools of Fine Art were organized at Cadiz, Valladolid and in the American provinces. The school founded by Antonio Viladomat at Barcelona was the only one to keep a clearly marked character of its own; this was due to the independence of its promoter, who adhered to the XVIIth-century tradition of religious painting, at once Baroque and realistic.

In the lists of the founders, prizemen and directors of the Academy we find the names of Pernicharo, Antonio Gonzalez Velazquez, Antonio Melendez, José del Castillo, Mariano Salvador Maella and Francisco Bayeu; Goya figures only as an unsuccessful candidate. In

any case the most interesting painters were those who worked in isolation. The large output of Luiz Melendez, Antonio's son, consisted almost entirely of still lifes, though on occasion he did some excellent portraits. The limitations of his art, its coldness and meticulousness, differentiate it both from the traditional 'bodegones' and the still lifes of Chardin, his contemporary. Yet he has a rare sense of volumes and his stiff precision is impressive in its way. Another curious artist is Luis Paret, who illustrated the fashions and picturesque aspects of the world around him, and owed much to a French artist, La Traverse, a friend of Boucher, who spent some time at the French Embassy. Paret painted scenes of public rejoicings, seaports and genre pieces, with a lively sense of humor and an appropriate technique of rapid brushstrokes, light, translucent colors. Lastly, a quite amazing portraitist appeared on the scene, Joaquin Inza, whose work recalls Goya's early portraits.

But the true art leaders still were foreigners. Charles III had brought with him from Naples Raphael Mengs, then at the height of his renown as a classicist 'reformer,' all for Greek perfection. For ten years Mengs played the part of a dictator, backed by the Academy which he had under his thumb. None the less the King had recourse to the most effective antidote imaginable for Mengs's staid academicism, when he called in Tiepolo to paint the ceilings of the Palace of the Orient, lavishing on them the sunset glory of Venetian color-magic. It is interesting to note that besides these major works, Tiepolo bequeathed to the world his *Caprices*, curious sketches in which he recorded his impressions of the oddities of human conduct. And meanwhile, in that humble, but tenacious art center, Saragossa, where the future of Spanish art was in the making, young Goya was growing up to manhood.

LUIS MELENDEZ (1716-1780). BODEGON : MELON AND PEARS. (15¾ × 20″)
MUSEUM OF FINE ARTS, BOSTON.

GOYA

★

NEO-CLASSICISM AND ROMANTICISM

THE IMITATORS OF GOYA

IMPRESSIONISM AND EXPRESSIONISM

FRANCISCO GOYA (1746-1828). THE BLIND GUITARIST, 1778. DETAIL. PRADO, MADRID.

GOYA

BECAUSE Goya died in France in the heyday of Romanticism and because he was in deep spiritual communion (personal contact being impossible owing to his old age and infirmities) with this new movement that he had foreshadowed and foreseen, and which was so well in keeping with his 'legend' and his personality—for all these reasons we are apt to forget that Goya was primarily and essentially a man of the XVIIIth century. During his last phase he explored domains of art so new and strange that our age may well believe itself the first to understand their purport. Actually, however, Goya proves, by his mere existence, that in the XVIIIth century there were present no less all the elements of the modern way of seeing than of our modern way of thinking.

Goya inherited a vast legacy from the past, nor did he abjure it. To his mind, the large-scale religious composition of Baroque art was far from having spent its driving force, and provincial realism had retained its solid merits. He was no less interested in technical procedures, past and present than in the contributions made by the French and English schools and in the tenets (formulated in Spain later than elsewhere) of a meticulous academicism. But a day came when the veil of appearances was shattered ; Goya discovered Man, essential Man, microcosm of the rhythms and structure of the Cosmos. Thus the pattern of his art was transfigured by the irruption of his own personality ; he imposed on it an accent of truth that played havoc with the accepted rules. This is why we seem to feel Goya's presence behind all the great emancipating movements; we feel him in Delacroix, in Daumier and in Manet—and in the XXth century he would certainly not be ill at ease.

A great decorator and an objective painter of the Court of the Bourbons in its last stage of decay, Goya was more, far more than this ; he passionately recorded the 'disasters,' the 'caprices' and the 'absurdities' of the world, and he was also the painter of the 'Deaf Man's House,' one of those rare artists who have delved deep into the mysteries of the subconscious and the dream. And when we also recall the psychological insight of his portraits and his pungent renderings of the varied aspects of the life around him, it seems almost incredible that one single man should have covered so much ground in but half a century.

Goya came of humble parents. In after life, however, he laid claim to noble descent, claimed that his mother, Gracia Lucientes, was a titled lady, and took to inserting the aristocratic French *de* into his name and signing 'Francisco de Goya.' (But we must not forget that sometimes he humorously wrote ' Francisco de los Toros'—which maybe, in the last analysis, is as good a title as anyone could wish for.) His father, son of a notary, after working as a gilder at Saragossa, had migrated to a small country village, Fuendetodos, where his wife owned a piece of ground ; the cottage where the artist was born is now a venerated place of pilgrimage. If this poverty-stricken hamlet, in its barren, treeless, riverless setting, still makes so deep an impression on the visitor this is because it is so characteristic of the province which was always dear to Goya's heart. No region is so typically Spanish as the Province of Aragon, that central basin of the Ebro, ringed round with lofty mountains, swept by bitter winds, seared by the fires of the summer sun. From this iron soil a hardy race has wrung a bare existence century after century, and nothing, neither unfriendly nature nor the presence of invading armies, has ever tamed their proud, indomitable spirit. Until he was fourteen Goya led the normal life of the children of the shepherds and peasants of his native village. But he soon displayed a talent for art and painted for the village church a picture of Nuestra Señora del Pilar, patroness of Aragon.

In 1760 Goya's father returned to Saragossa and resumed his trade there. Goya was sent to the Escuela Pia, where the master was Father Joaquin (the designation ' Escuela Pia ' applies to schools kept up by the Ignorantine Friars), and while at school made friends with Martin Zapater. Soon after, he began studying with José Luzan, a local artist. Francisco Bayeu, somewhat older, after studying under the same master had obtained a scholarship enabling him to spend two years in Madrid, and Goya's one desire was to follow in his footsteps.

In January 1763 Raphael Mengs summoned Bayeu to Madrid and in the fall of the same year Goya, greatly daring, migrated to the capital. But luck was against him and he failed to obtain a scholarship from the Academy of San Fernando. Nothing is known of his doings until 1766, when he sat again for the examination—and failed again. Four years later Goya, who meanwhile had gone to Italy and apparently stayed some time in Rome, was awarded a second prize in the competitive examination of the Academy of Fine Arts at Parma. With reference to this incident, a writer in the *Moniteur de France*, after describing the picture, declares that Goya would have come out first had he kept closer to his subject and taken more trouble to make his colors accurate. By the end of 1771 he was back in Saragossa, where he was commissioned by the Board of Works of the Del Pilar Cathedral to decorate the small choir, a task which he disposed of quickly. Next, he was employed on painting a series of large murals for the Carthusian Monastery of Aula Dei (near Saragossa), on mural decorations at the Sobrediel Palace and on paintings for the Church of Remolinos. About 1773 Goya returned to Madrid where he now worked in collaboration with Bayeu, whose sister Josefa he soon after married. By her he had a son early in 1777. Bayeu and Goya had already begun designing for the royal tapestry-factory, the former in 1775, the latter in 1776.

Actually our information regarding these fifteen formative years of Goya's career is scanty. To get an idea of this early phase we must refer to the first fully authenticated works. It is probably not so much a question of trying to determine what influences Goya underwent, as one of ascertaining the characteristics of the various *milieux* in which he moved during these early years. Far oftener than not an artist's personality is shaped not so much by direct visual experience of others' works as by his efforts to respond to certain tendencies, as yet unformulated, that are vaguely 'in the air.' Thus at the beginning of the XVIIth century the tendencies we associate with the name of Caravaggio made themselves felt everywhere, even in places to which his pictures had not had time to make their way, and we apply the epithet 'Caravaggesque' to many, often very diverse, ventures into new fields of art. So far as Goya is concerned, his individual genius was slow in maturing and it seems certain that in his early days he was far from rebelling against his environment, though he kept open house to new ideas, was eager to explore the less frequented technical byways— engraving processes, frescos and the like—and, in fact, picked up whatever scraps of useful information came his way. This did not, however, prevent him from striking out for himself as well. In the biographical summary which he compiled himself for inclusion in the 'Guide' to the Prado (1828), with reference to the first of his pictures, a *Portrait of Queen Maria Luisa on Horseback*, to be exhibited there, he mentioned that he had studied for four years under José Luzan, who had taught him drawing and had him copy the best prints in his possession. But he was careful to add that until he went to Rome he always painted " out of his own head," and his only masters were his personal observation and the famous pictures to be seen in Rome and Spain.

José Luzan, whose instruction he seems to dismiss so lightly, had lived in Naples, where he worked with a disciple of Solimena and Luca Giordano. On his return to Saragossa he set up a studio which was frequented by the Bayeus, Vallespin and Goya. His religious paintings are said to be commendable. But there were other notable artists in the capital of Aragon at this time. Enrique Lafuente Ferrari has made it clear that there had existed for a long time a flourishing Aragonese school, linking up with the best traditions of the past by way of Jusepe Martinez, the friend of Ribera and Velazquez. Antonio Martinez, Jusepe's son who had gone with his father to Italy had painted at the Monastery of Aula Dei, where Goya later worked, no less than forty-eight pictures, remarkable for the spontaneity and boldness of their execution. There were also the Rabiellas; the father, painter of battle-pieces, being a sort of Aragonese Valdés Leal, and the son, a religious painter on the lines of Luca Giordano, who made some decorations in the Cathedral and the Del Pilar Church. Though Baroque influences were still strong, the new ideas in art were not frowned on; thus Pernicharo, an Aragonese, studied under the French artist Houasse in Madrid. Invited on his return from Rome to paint the dome of the Del Pilar Church, a painter from Madrid,

FRANCISCO GOYA (1746-1828). BLIND MAN'S BUFF, 1791. (105 ½ × 137 ½")
PRADO, MADRID.

Antonio Gonzalez Velazquez, had produced a work in the best academic manner. This was in 1753 and next year proposals were made for establishing an academy of art at Saragossa. (This project was not carried out until 1782, with the foundation of the Academy of San Luis.) Finally, soon after Mengs' coming to Spain, a Bohemian painter, Merklein, had opened a studio in Saragossa. He was the teacher of Francisco Bayeu, who had already imbibed from Gonzalez Velazquez the rudiments of his dry, scrupulously 'correct' style. Bayeu, who had married Merklein's daughter, was sent by his father-in-law to work under Mengs.

Francisco Bayeu cuts the figure of the leader of the small group of young painters at Saragossa, its other members being his brothers and Goya. Cean speaks of his pride and crotchetiness. None the less Goya was impressed, if somewhat grudgingly, by his cold, accurate painting and painstaking drawing, thanks to which he had won success and prompt admission to the Academy of Madrid. Francisco Bayeu readily assimilated that technique of an objective approach to the model and the meticulous exactitude which were Mengs' chief assets and, like his master, proved to be an excellent portrait-painter. Despite the part he played in the renovation of the royal tapestry-factory, his tapestry cartoons form the most conventional and least satisfying part of his output ; they are far from having the poetic qualities and freedom of Paret, who was the true pioneer in this field. Ramon Bayeu, of the same age as Goya, was far inferior to Francisco. There was yet a third brother, Manuel, a monk and an original, independent-minded painter, who was one of Goya's lifelong friends.

Mengs was dictator of the art world of Madrid when Goya settled there. Actually, the Mengs régime was not so dessicating as has often been alleged ; his theory of neo-classicism contained a judicious leaven of humanism, nor did he disdain the current trends of European art. Meanwhile German and Central European painters were furthering the creation of an ' international ' style of portrait ; we need only remember the part played by Zoffany in English portraiture. Through him and through others too—for there was close commercial intercourse with England, especially in the South—Spain came in contact with English painting, which at this time was making great forward strides, not only in the fields of landscape and genre but also in the interpretation of the human physiognomy. Though these tendencies were as yet only vaguely apprehended in Madrid, the work of the French painters (second-rank artists, it must be admitted) who had been called in by the Bourbons was a present reality. By a judicious collation of reproductions Sanchez Canton has proved that Goya's early work contains unmistakable reminiscences of the pictures of the life of the Spanish populace painted by Michel-Ange Houasse thirty years before—which are, in fact, anticipations of the famous tapestry cartoons. Also, in *St Francis Borgia and the Dying Impenitent*, painted by Goya in 1788 for the Cathedral of Valencia, the movements and gestures are obviously taken from Houasse's *St Francis Regis*. Few examples of the amazingly free work of the French pastel-painters had then reached Spain and the Spanish artists still kept to the old-style, somewhat pompous ' court portrait.' And this tradition, if tempered by the lightness and delicacy of German Rococo, lay at the origin of Goya's early portraits.

Lastly, in the course of his stay in Italy (of which, but for legends that grew up about his wild adventures, we know very little), Goya may well have found confirmation of the principles which had guided his early steps in art. As he himself has told us, he evidently saw many famous pictures, notably those by the Venetians, always so highly esteemed in Spain. Of the more recent artists it would appear to have been Magnasco from whom he learnt most. In his first religious works Goya drew inspiration from the bold, freely rendered forms of Luca Giordano, which had long since been taken over by the more provincial Spanish practitioners of decorative painting. Of more immediate interest is a habit which, following Magnasco and Tiepolo, Spanish painters were now acquiring, of painting preliminary sketches, synthetic, condensed versions of their subject, which in the analytic, detailed execution of the ' definitive ' picture lost the vibrant life and movement which had characterized the sketch. Over a long period Goya put the best of himself into these minor works, which enabled him to try his hand at successive variations on his favorite themes and indulge in personal experiments. Later on he ventured to impart this freedom of treatment to major works. It was probably from Italy—certainly not in Luzan's studio—that Goya acquired the technical basis of that skill in manipulating color which his inventive genius was to carry to such heights ; and to Italy, too, that he owed his knowledge of fresco-painting and his interest in the processes of engraving, then little known in Spain.

In later years, asked who were his masters, Goya replied : " I have had three masters: Velazquez, Rembrandt and Nature." In 1776 when he started working for the royal tapestry-factory, he knew nothing of the two first-named masters. As for the third, his new occupation was to bring him closely into touch with Nature. The craftsmen working in the Santa Barbara factory (founded in 1720 by Philip V) were inefficient, just capable of reproducing pallid imitations of Teniers. When, towards the end of the prosperous reign of Charles III, the First Minister Floridablanca was seeking to develop the luxury industries of Spain, it struck him that something might be done about the Santa Barbara factory ; surely improvements could be made in the quality of the work it turned out ? His first step was to put Mengs in charge, giving him a free hand, and to order the Flemish tapestry expert, Cornelius van der Goten, who looked after the production, to improve the technical equipment of the factory. It is all to the credit of Mengs that he had the good sense to enlist the best of the young painters in his team, and to have them supply compositions which, while in the tradition of the Flemish *bambocciate* and the French *scènes galantes*, were inspired by the colorful life of contemporary Madrid, its *fiestas* and the amusements of its populace.

The first cartoons were made by Francisco Bayeu, who at once set the tone and fixed the limits of the genre. Thereafter commissions were given to Ramon Bayeu, José del Castillo, Manuel Napoli and lastly Goya, who delivered his first composition, *La Merienda*, on October 30, 1776 ; next came the *La Florida Ball* on March 3, 1777, and on August 12 of the same year he handed in the *Affray at La Venta Nueva* and *The Maja and the Gallants*. To begin with it was almost a collective venture and the young artists' lack of experience in this field, coupled with the stereotyped methods of the weavers, resulted in productions that showed little genuine originality. In 1869, however, the discovery was made in a cellar of the Royal Palace at Madrid of a roll of 255 canvas 'models'—for actually these so-called cartoons are canvases— used at the Santa Barbara factory. Amongst them 43 are signed by Goya, and these are now on view at the Prado. Far better than the mediocre tapestries made 'after' them, they reveal to us the brilliancy of Goya's inspiration in its first state ; they also show that he soon outdistanced his colleagues and, by the same token, ranged far beyond the narrow field of tapestry designing. In the earliest cartoons we still find recalls of his pedestrian colleague Bayeu, who probably suggested the subjects to be treated and the way of treating them. But soon the cold, anaemic, conventional colors taken over from Mengs were replaced by a far richer palette, of boldly broken tints and warmer hues. In these Sambricio (in his *Goya's Tapestries*) sees the influence of Tiepolo who had spent his last ten years in Madrid and many examples of whose grandiose decorative work were to be seen there.

Quite probably the very restrictions involved in work of this order, the necessity, for instance, of using bright colors and omitting shadows, no less than the freedom ensured by

FRANCISCO GOYA (1746-1828). THE FIESTA OF SAN ISIDRO, 1788. DETAIL.
PRADO, MADRID.

FRANCISCO GOYA (1746-1828). PORTRAIT OF FRANCISCO BAYEU, 1786. (43 ½ × 32 ½")
SAN CARLOS MUSEUM, VALENCIA.

the rapid execution that was called for and the quest of movement *coûte que coûte*, served Goya as so many means of testing his painterly resources and limbering up his technique. Though bound by the conventional arrangement of his figures that was imposed on him, he introduced unusual foreshortenings due less, no doubt, to direct observation than to a wish to stress individual peculiarities. Moreover, since the themes of the cartoons were ' by order ' to be taken from the life of the day (into which Goya, intoxicated by his early success, had plunged exuberantly), he was able to step up the sentimental scenes he was forced to paint to a level of expressiveness violent to the point of truculence. Mindful of the texture of tapestry, he juxtaposed patches of vivid color instead of laying in his pigment in smooth broad planes, thus imparting to the picture surface a curious power of suggestion. Indeed some of the faces, built up with a thick impasto, have the hallucinating quality of his later work ; an example is his *Blind Guitarist*. They stand out emphatically from the crowd of conventional supernumeraries necessitated by the rules of the genre, which called for landscapes usually far too large and ill proportioned, rather like inferior stage scenery. (It is another proof of Goya's precocious artistry that he contrived to impart such subtle atmospheric variations to these stereotyped backgrounds.) His best cartoons are those in which the subject has least importance, and which show figures singly or in small groups, such as the *Tobacco Guard*, or the scene of two masons carrying a wounded mate. Seldom, except in some satirical works, do we find any lingering over details or any actual likeness ; Goya concentrates on the broad, overall effect. Similarly the preliminary sketches of his first religious works are, for the period, unconventional, and the same is true of his drawings, in which he wastes no time on any detailed analysis of his subjects but relies on his first, general impression—so much so that it is almost impossible to identify the models.

This period of painting tapestry cartoons (it lasted until 1791) enabled Goya to build up a vast repertory of forms, on which he drew throughout his life. Even while engaged on them, he sometimes used them as *data* for sketches and for pictures commissioned from him. Thus, at the request of the Duke of Osuna, he painted a suite of twenty-three rustic or genre scenes for his country house, the Alameda ; in some of these we see his earliest ventures into the realm of the fantastic. In *The Fiesta of San Isidro*, a picture painted for his own satisfaction in 1787, which he did not sell until twelve years later, he seems to aim at synthesizing the essentials of his discoveries. This small canvas includes a panoramic view of Madrid, with its steeples and the big cubic masses of its palaces. The river flows right through the composition, bisecting it horizontally. On the near side of the river, facing the city bathed in mellow light, is the vast meadow flanking the Manzanares, crowded with a dark, seething throng of merrymakers, many of them indicated by a single stroke. Close up in the foreground, which is ingeniously tilted up on either side of the picture, are type-figures of the ' Goyesque ' world, brilliantly illuminated.

Henceforward these type-figures are often to be seen in the large religious pictures Goya continued painting. As with the tapestry cartoons, he thought up his own versions of the time-honored themes and, greatly daring, interpreted them on ' modern ' lines, thus doing as Rembrandt had done before him (and as, later, Delacroix was to do) : breathing new life into a genre that, after the way of genres, was lapsing into a dry-as-dust convention. In so doing he broke not only with the classical compositional rules of the academies, but also with the impersonal Baroque construction which had acted as the scaffolding of his first pictures. In fact he handles sacred subjects exactly as if he were painting scenes of every-day life, though without limiting himself to the factual. For he excels in conjuring up celestial or demonic beings, whose curious convincingness and air of palpable reality owes much to the matter-of-fact settings in which they are located. In this respect the two big pictures he painted for the Chapel of the Dukes of Osuna in the Cathedral of Valencia (in 1788), the *Farewell of St Francis Borgia* and *St Francis Borgia and the Dying Impenitent*, mark a turning-point ; indeed they may be regarded as a prelude to modern religious painting. Especially in the second picture the painter's boldness is nothing short of amazing and he succeeds in depicting with equal realism the convulsed body of the dying man, the fiends looming up beside the deathbed and the celestial radiance emanating from the saint. The Primitives, too, had a way of treating earth, heaven and hell as if on the same plane ; their meticulously realistic portrayals stemmed from the visible world, whose diverse appearances and values they were careful to retain. Zurbaran proceeded on similar lines, though he also aimed at bringing out the hidden life of men and things. El Greco alone had an intuitive awareness of the Other World and all his work is bathed in a supernatural light. But the Spanish religious painters who came later were content with creating a sacrosanct world that was purely a matter of convention, inspired by reality yet lacking the immediacy of the real, since it purported to be outside Time. Then, at long last, Goya rediscovered the virtues of the here-and-now. From 1788 on all his religious works—and including as they do the decoration of Santa Cueva at Cadiz, of San Antonio de la Florida, *Judas betraying Christ* in the Cathedral of Toledo and the pictures in the Church of San Anton at Madrid, they are not to be disre-garded—strike a note of modernity *à outrance*. Thus in the La Florida picture of a dead man being recalled to life by St Anthony of Padua, the spectators of the miracle are a typical Madrid crowd, colorful and exuberant. Similarly, in the Toledo picture (the most Rembrand-tesque of Goya's works), the faces of those surrounding Christ are frankly vulgar.

Nevertheless, Goya cannot be accused of dragging down sacred themes to a crudely terrestrial level, as was done, for reasons of their own, by so many of his predecessors. It is truer to say that, by the sheer intensity of a realism keyed up to its highest pitch, he imparts an amazingly concrete objectivity to the subjective and the supernatural. Thus, paradoxically enough, his religious pictures, in the very boldness of their technical innovations, the violence of their contrasts and foreshortenings, seem to link up with those highly personal works of his which aim at freeing men from superstition and the specters of their imagin-ation. Actually the religious and the iconoclastic are but different facets of the same creative impulse, and here we have another example of the many-sidedness of Goya's *Weltanschauung*. It enabled him to reconcile the humanitarian, rationalistic concepts of the ' natural religion ' popularized by contemporary philosophy, with survivals of that passionate religiosity which slumbers in the heart of every Spaniard—and sometimes finds expression in downright blasphemy. No other artist has ever made the monstrous spawn of the underworld of the human consciousness, so amazingly *alive*. In his seemingly most anti-religious works—for example, his processions of Flagellants and Inquisition scenes—he himself seems to be overcome by a sort of religious frenzy ; indeed we feel he has an instinctive sympathy with these manifestations of a crude, instinctive piety. And so tellingly does he depict them that the movements of the figures, the feverish rhythms of the lights and darks tend to arouse in the observer something of the demented ecstasy of the participants. Stranger still, this same effect is produced even when facial distortions and grotesque accessories show that the painter's intent was mainly satirical.

Thanks to his employment in the tapestry factory Goya had access to the royal collec-tions, which contained the masterpieces of Spanish art as well as the fine Flemish and Italian pictures acquired by several generations of Spanish Kings. Thus Goya ' discovered ' Velazquez, and in token of his admiration he copied, first in pen-and-ink, then with the etching needle, eighteen of Velazquez' most famous works. There is no question that the lessons of his great predecessor had a decisive influence in shaping his technique at this stage and that he also now became more aware of the need for overall unity in a composition. In his last tapestry cartoons the subjects are better integrated into the setting, while the brushstrokes are more fluent. Probably it was the example of Velazquez that encouraged Goya to try his hand at portrait-painting. This happened somewhat later than might have been expected, and once again it was the circumstances of his life that led him to explore a new field of art. He began by painting his patrons : Van der Goten, Floridablanca, the Infante Don Luis and his family—this last an interesting first essay in group portraiture. Despite his lack of experience Goya made a point of posing his models in an appropriate setting and indicating their social status. He placed himself in a corner of the composition, standing at his easel or else in a dim light presenting a picture to his patron. The fact that these pictures were not a success

FRANCISCO GOYA (1746-1828). COUNTESS DEL CARPIO, MARCHIONESS DE LA SOLANA, 1791. (72×48¾″)
DE BESTEIGUI COLLECTION, BIARRITZ.

did not prevent his persisting in the path which was to lead to such masterpieces as *King Charles IV and his Family*. Similarly in 1783 in the huge *Preaching of St Bernardino of Siena* (San Francisco el Grande, Madrid) he inserted himself among the figures on the right of the picture, in almost the same attitude as that of his first self-portrait (in the Museum of Agen), which bears the same date. In the last-named work we see the painter wearing a dark cloak, and his massive, forceful head with its shock of hair tossed back and the full, self-confident face stand out against a light-hued background. Though usually assigned to the year 1787, the small canvas in the Count de Villagonzalo's collection does not seem much later than the portrait described above. In it Goya is seen painting, solidly planted in front of his canvas in an almost bellicose posture. He is wearing skin-tight breeches with horizontal stripes, a short embroidered coat, gaudy as a torero's, and a ' stove-pipe ' hat having a metal brim with fixtures for holding candles. (Girodet is said to have used headgear of this kind for painting at night.) Above a white ruffle the rather grim face stares straight at the spectator; little can be seen of it except the piercing eyes, thick lips and unkempt hair, since Goya has placed himself in a rather unpromising position, with his back to a window. Though he is looking away, the brush in his right hand is resting on the canvas, while the left holds forth a palette speckled with little dabs of pure colors. Already Goya shows an almost miraculous skill in painting garments. The general effect of this picture is one of juvenile exuberance; that of a young man thrilled to feel himself one of the elect company of painters.

But Goya's great wish was for official recognition. As early as 1779 he had been presented to King Charles III and his children, the Prince of Asturias and Princess Maria Luisa. The royal family treated him with much kindness and he was soon on those easy terms with the younger members of the House which enabled him in later years to take such liberties when painting them. As then was customary, Goya's first royal portraits were based on documentation but before long he was allowed to have his models sit for him, and he now made it his aim to tell the truth about this exalted world whose flaws he was quick to perceive. In 1786 he painted *Charles III in Hunting Costume*, keeping closely to Velazquez' methods. After the death of King Charles III (December, 1788), his rise was rapid. Next April that uncouth, good-natured sovereign Charles IV gave him the post of Court Painter, which meant that he was required to act as curator of the royal collections and also to add to them likenesses of the new rulers. He soon became wealthy, and the royal favor he enjoyed opened to him the doors of even the most exclusive homes of the aristocracy. The society portraits he now turned out were admirable, despite the conventional poses, for the delicacy of their execution and the artist's skillful renderings of the sheen of costumes in a range of pearly greys. It was now, too, that he made the portrait of the Marchioness of Pontejos, giving it a mannered elegance more in keeping with Marie Antoinette's Versailles than with contemporary Spain or the *milieu* of his patrons, the Duke and Duchess of Osuna. In this phase he set technique before expression. Nevertheless in the last-named work the banality of the composition is redeemed by the curious effect of the eyes of the persons represented, arranged like notes on a stave of music.

Goya had already made the acquaintance of the Duchess of Alba and in the summer of 1786 he stayed at Piedrahita, near Avila, the country house of the Duke and Duchess. It was probably here he painted the *Grape-Harvest* cartoon, the locale of which has been identified in this region. Apparently his relations with his hostess were at this time purely friendly; not until several years later is there mention of the celebrated liaison between the painter and the Duchess. On the contrary this is the period during which we have most information about his married life. In 1784 his wife bore him a son, Javier, the only one of his many children who did not die young. The old story of his having had twenty children is a wild exaggeration; scrutiny of the Register of Births at Madrid has reduced the total to five. In August 1790 Goya took his wife to Valencia, on her doctor's advice, for the sea air.

Towards the end of 1792 Goya went to Cadiz, where he painted the portrait of his friend Sebastian Martinez. The story that the Duchess accompanied him on this trip has no foundation in fact. On his way back Goya fell seriously ill at Seville and he returned to Cadiz for a

lengthy course of treatment, staying with his friend Martinez. In a letter of March, 1793, to Pedro Arascot, Martinez wrote: " Goya wanted to write you a long letter, but I would not let him, as I knew how this would affect his head, where all his trouble lies. " To Zapater he wrote : " Goya is slightly better, but progress is sadly slow. The noises in his head and his deafness have not passed away ; however, his sight has improved and he no longer has fits of dizziness and can walk up and down stairs without difficulty." After examining these letters Dr Blanco y Soler rejects the view, hitherto generally accepted, that Goya's disease was of a syphilitic order. He points out that if he had contracted such a malady at the age of forty-seven it would have been almost impossible for him to continue living and working normally up to the age of eighty. Dr Blanco y Soler considers that the symptoms described point to an inflammation of the nervous structures in the ' labyrinth ' of the ear, i.e. the disease known as neurolabyrinthitis.

Goya got over this attack but it left him stone deaf. Cut off from the sounds of the outside world, all he now heard were his inner voices, and henceforth they were ever with him. There was nothing for it but to make a complete break with all his former habits, and he now took stock of his inner resources and such few consolations as life still held out to him. For he realized the isolation to which his deafness had condemned him but also what his imagination stood to gain by this. In 1794 he wrote : " My health is neither better nor worse ; there are moments when I am so furious with everything that I hate myself as well ; others when I feel relatively calm." And elsewhere he writes : " So as to turn my mind from brooding over my misfortunes and also to meet some part of the heavy expenses due to my illness, I have now embarked on a series of easel pictures, in which I am able to include that personal observation which has usually to be ruled out in commissioned works, where so little scope can be given to caprice and invention."

It may well have been a feeling of compassion for Goya's sad lot, now that his deafness had cut him off from the gay life of Madrid, that moved the Duchess of Alba to make so much of him. Born in 1762, Teresa Cayetana Maria del Pilar, thirteenth Duchess of Alba, was the last of a noble line. Her husband, Luis de Villafranca—who by letters patent was given the title of the Duke of Alba—was a rather gloomy, sickly, stay-at-home man, whose one interest in life was music. (Goya painted him leaning on his harpsichord, with a score by Haydn in front of him.) As might be expected, his personality was completely overshadowed by that of his wife, who from her girlhood was famed for her beauty, wit and willfulness. Brought up on the lines laid down in *Emile*, by a father who was a fervent admirer of the Encyclopedists, she had—unlike the Spanish girls of her *milieu*, educated on traditional lines—come to regard it as quite normal to gratify any desire that came to her, without troubling about ' appearances.' Quick on the uptake, she had acquired, almost effortlessly, much knowledge of the science and philosophy of the day, but her temperament remained at once fiery, haughty and sensual—in a word, typically Spanish. In the best chapters of his somewhat novelistic *Life of Goya*, Eugenio d'Ors draws attention to certain traits in the character of the Duchess which were symptoms of the *mal du siècle*, developing at this period, which led the nobility to waive their privileges and champion the people, men of high culture to yearn for the condition of the " noble savage " and great ladies to demean themselves by way of expiation for some imaginary guilt. At the Trianon the Queen of France was playing at being a simple shepherdess ; in Madrid the nobility played at being *majos* or *toreros*. The Duchess of Alba yielded (all too readily, as one of the *Caprichos* bitterly makes plain) to men of a different class from hers ; she took into her household freaks, dwarfs and buffoons, and amongst her *protégés* were the ugliest specimens of humanity she could collect : an old, lame, one-eyed monk and the half-wit Benito. Also, she doted on children, her special pets being the son of a servant and a little negress, Maria de la Luz. All forms of physical degradation, perhaps because of their suggestions of the primitive, appealed to her.

The large full-length portrait of the Duchess of Alba with a landscape background is dated 1795. The portrait of her husband poring over his music belongs to the same year. On June 9, 1796, the Duke died and the Duchess retired to Andalusia for a period of mourning.

FRANCISCO GOYA (1746-1828). THE DUCHESS OF ALBA, 1795. (76¼×51″)
COLLECTION OF THE DUKE OF ALBA, MADRID.

FRANCISCO GOYA (1746-1828). SELF-PORTRAIT, 1785. (16½ × 9¾")
COLLECTION OF THE COUNT OF VILLAGONZALO, MADRID.

Goya is known to have been away from Madrid at this time and it seems certain he accompanied her. Two sketch-books contain records of this stay in Andalusia. The second portrait of the Duchess, wearing a mantilla, was probably also made at San Lucar, since she did not return to Madrid during that year. In these sketch-books and the two portraits we have the so to speak documentary evidence of a love-affair whose secret was so well guarded that even today the historian has to fall back on conjecture. In the first portrait (in the Duke of Alba's collection) the Duchess is standing in front of a landscape stretching far away into the distance ; the proud erectness of her attitude is haloed as it were by a filmy dress that floats around her, extending to the ground. The clean-cut face, framed in a cascade of black hair, contrasts with the soft whites and greys, intersected by a red belt, of the drapery. But it is a detail, the right hand, that above all grips our attention. Hands play an important part in all Goya's portraits (he went so far as to omit them in minor works and in commissions that he judged inadequately remunerated) and in a somewhat primitive but none the less effective way they indicate the personality of the sitter. A painter is shown holding a brush, an architect a set-square, a singer or music-lover a musical score, a pretty woman a flower. Floridablanca's hand is toying with his spectacles ; kings in hunting dress hold their guns like mechanized sceptres, marchionesses flirt a fan. In the case of one hand alone, Goya abandons these conventional referents : that of the Duchess of Alba, whose gesture seems to be stressing a command and pointing, seconded by an imperious gaze, towards the inscription on a flagstone beside her : *To the Duchess of Alba, Francisco Goya.* Symbolical details count far too much in Goya's work for this to be ignored. It is no less revealing than the detail of the 1797 portrait (Hispanic Society, New York) in which the Duchess is wearing two rings, one bearing the name ' Goya,' the other ' Alba.'

Further records of Goya's stay in Andalusia are to be found in the sketch-books preserved in the Prado. They are incomplete ; the large album has six pages in all, a smaller sketch-book five pages ; the sketches, in Indian ink, are on both sides of the pages ; thus there are twenty-two in all, arranged in two alternating series. In the first the Duchess is easily identifiable, " surprised," " in despair," " with the little negro child in her arms," " wearing a mantilla," " sitting on a bank beside the road " ; also, in the big album, " with a soldier," " in a swoon, perhaps," " on a visit," " out for a walk." The second series, much more freely treated, shows a woman of a quite different physical type. Also belonging to this period are two small pictures dated 1795 of the Duchess, her duenna and the little negress.

It would seem that the happiest period of the love-affair between the artist and his mistress was that of the years covered by these records, 1795-1797. However, the liaison continued until the death, under mysterious circumstances, of the Duchess, on July 23, 1802. (There were whispers of her having been poisoned as a result of the Queen's jealousy of her.) But after 1797 a change came over their relations. Two etchings in the *Caprichos* series, one of which was not made public until many years later, show that these took the course that, given the temperament of Goya's mistress, was but to be expected. In *Volaverunt* we see a woman, unmistakably the Duchess, being carried away by three witches, the face of one of whom is said to be that of the Matador Romero. The unissued *Capricho, Vision of Fickleness and Falsehood,* is even more explicit. The Duchess has two faces crowned with butterflies' wings. One of them is turned towards Goya who stretches out his arms ; the other towards a man pressing his hand to his lips. On the death of the Duchess Goya designed a mural for the chapel where she was buried. In his sketch the dead woman's body is being carried by three hooded figures—an obvious recall of *Volaverunt.*

On his return to Madrid in the spring of 1796 Goya flung himself into his work with the desperate ardor of a man determined to prove that illness has not sapped his energy. Though he resigned his post of Director of the Academy on the ground that he was " now so deaf that he could hear absolutely nothing, not even the loudest noises," he undertook some large-scale works : the decorations at La Florida and the series of *Caprichos.* He also painted portraits of his friends Melendez Valdes, Martin Zapater and Bernardo Iriarte ; in 1798

of General Urrutia, the French Ambassador Guillemardet and the Minister of State Jovellanos; in 1799 of Moratin, the Marquis of Bondad Real, the Marchioness of Lazan, the Marchioness of Santiago, the singer Lorenza Carrea ; in 1800 of the Countess of Chinchon. In these portraits Goya followed two methods which ended up by coalescing. In painting the faces of his friends he kept to a strictly psychological approach, that is to say he ruled out all non-essentials and embellishments, and went straight to the heart of his subject. Hence the objective realism of these portraits and their insistence on expression. In the more ' official ' portraits, however, he had recourse to every method of evocation and suggestion ; significant details and accessories abound and even the most trivial features of the model's costume play a part. Thus by the very richness of the *matière* Goya succeeded in imparting interest to even the dullest, least rewarding models. He was at his most inspired when painting women; none of Goya's works has more poetic feeling than his renderings of the supple grace of the Marchioness of Lazan and the pathetic charm of the Countess of Chinchon, daughter of the Infante Don Luis and the much wronged wife of Godoy, Charles's favorite minister. Goya had known her as a little girl, before the Queen had so heartlessly arranged her marriage to the worthless royal favorite. We see her as a tiny forlorn figure lost in the vastness of the composition, yet what holds our eyes is the painter's rendering of the sumptuous garments —never has the aerial lightness of his brush shown itself to happier effect—and sadness is transmuted into beauty. We are conscious here of Goya's deep humanity ; his struggles with the monsters of his imagination did not harden his heart, and all his life long he showed compassion for the weak and the suffering of the earth. He had a special tenderness for children; in his harshly realistic group portraits of the royal house, those effigies of pompous futility, only the children are handled leniently.

Meanwhile Goya was solidly established in Court favor. In 1799 he was summoned to the Granja to make two portraits of Queen Maria Luisa—in one he painted her riding her horse ' Martial,' in the other wearing a mantilla—and she was equally delighted with both. On October 30 he was appointed First Court Painter, with a large salary and a private carriage. He now painted the *Charles IV on Horseback*. He often went to Aranjuez to stay with Godoy, who had learnt to converse with him by signs. In 1800, just after finishing the portrait of the Countess of Chinchon, he was bidden by the King to Aranjuez to paint a picture " of all of us together." In four trips he had blocked out the individual poses and the general arrangement of the group ; also he made separate, detailed studies of each of the thirteen figures. He grouped all these people in the simplest possible manner, with the royal couple in the center, the Queen being given the most salient place. Between the King and Queen stands the small Infante Francisco de Paula, with a line of shadow just above him. The effect is to divide the composition into two distinct parts : in that on the right, consisting of the King, his brother and his son, warm colors, red and gold, predominate ; in the left-hand section, the Queen, her daughter, daughter-in-law and that owlish old maid, the Infanta Maria Josefa, are painted in cool tones, with blue and silver predominating. But simple as the general lay-out may be, there is a quite amazing *finesse* in the rendering of each and every detail. Goya was now at the zenith of his technical proficiency ; it would be impossible to go farther in the rendering of the vibrant sheen of colors, the play of sudden gleams and broken lights, without running the risk of lapsing into artifice. In any case, after this dazzling feat of virtuosity, Goya began to move away little by little from these procedures. Despite its expressive power, this picture is full of subtlety and nuances. We should probably be wrong in reading into it any satirical intent ; Goya painted just what he saw, and was obviously delighted by the glow and glitter of the costumes and decorations. Nor are the faces caricatures ; they are objective descriptions, so skillful and so accurate that even their ' victims ' expressed entire satisfaction with the painter's work.

Meanwhile, however, a great change had been coming over Goya's outlook on life, which revealed itself even in his features. The self-portrait etched in 1799 and prefixed to the *Caprichos* shows a prematurely aged, wry-mouthed, morose man. His way of dressing, too, has changed ; he no longer wears gay colors, but prefers blacks and greys. Already he has taken to wearing a tall, shaggy top-hat, a first version of that bell-shaped hat known as a ' Bolivar ' which was to make him a conspicuous figure at Bordeaux in later days. After the Duchess of Alba's death Goya seems to have gone through another phase of deep depression ; his production slowed up and next to nothing is known of his life at this time. However now and again he added to his wonderful gallery of portraits. To meet the wishes of his sitters, he often gave them heroic or impressive poses ; the Marchioness of Santa Cruz is shown holding a lyre, Don Felix de Azara in the attitude of a military commander, Godoy in that of a victorious general after a great battle, amongst flags and trophies. Here the warmth and vigor of the colors more than redeem the triteness of the lay-out.

In most of Goya's portraits of this period, however, the treatment of the figures is much less conventional. Even when his sitters are grandees, such as the Count Fernan Nuñez or the Marquis of San Adrian, their romantic poses express their inmost selves far more than their rank or functions. This is particularly noticeable in his portraits of women, those for instance of the Marchioness of Espeja, Doña Antonia Zareta and Doña Isabel Cobos de Porcel ; here Goya applies himself to rendering the temperaments, even the secret passions, of his sitters, and resolutely dispenses with accessories. *A fortiori*, when painting his personal friends (for example, Maiquez the actor), he displays ever increasing boldness and freedom. At this time the evolution of his art was extraordinarily rapid ; soon he quite dispensed

FRANCISCO GOYA (1746-1828). THE FAMILY OF CHARLES IV, 1800. (110 × 132″)
PRADO, MADRID.

FRANCISCO GOYA (1746-1828). QUEEN MARIA LUISA ON HORSEBACK, 1799. (131 ½ × 109″)
PRADO, MADRID.

with backgrounds and details and often dashed his color on to the canvas with a finger or his palette-knife, in his haste to record the inspiration of the moment.

All Goya's work is stamped by the successive crises of his life, each of which quickened powers beneath the threshold of his consciousness and speeded up his artistic development, which but for them would have been slow and laborious. The first shock was of a physical nature : the sudden loss of his hearing in 1793. The second was the death of the Duchess of Alba, in 1802. Then, in 1808, came a disaster of a national order which shook Goya to the very core of his being, more intensely than even the severest illness. It befell when Goya was passing through a phase of uncertainty ; almost we might say he was marking time. Though his home was in the heart of Madrid (at 9, Puerta del Sol), he was living as a recluse, having long since broken off relations with the Court and the world of fashion. Gradually he had ceased painting portraits and was turning to scenes of contemporary life, more general in their application ; also, he was contemplating another series of *Caprichos*. It was now that, out of the blue so to speak, came the French invasion and he found himself forced to take sides, no easy matter given the political conditions of the time.

For when the French troops entered Spain, the Spanish populace welcomed them as liberators ; there was a general uprising, the King was forced to abdicate and his son Ferdinand VII declared King amid general rejoicings. But this did not suit Napoleon's book ; he wished to do away with the absolute monarchy and the superstitions that were cramping the life of Spain, and to integrate the country into the new enlightened Europe of his dream. He guessed — and rightly — that he could not count on the co-operation of the new king, who was as narrow-minded as the worst of his predecessors. Accordingly he summoned Ferdinand to Bayonne, where Charles IV had already taken refuge. Reluctantly and against the advice of his First Minister Urquijo, Ferdinand complied. Meanwhile feelings ran high in Madrid, where French troops now were stationed. On May 2, when the populace demonstrated against the departure of the little Infante Francisco de Paula to Bayonne, Murat dispersed the crowd by force, and now that the train was fired, rioting broke out in all parts of the city and attacks were made on isolated French soldiers, while the Spanish troops, though remaining in their barracks, supplied the insurgents with arms. Order was restored only by charges of the ' Mamelukes ' after what amounted to pitched battles in the streets. That night, overriding Murat's instructions, General Grouchy ordered the summary execution of certain members of the uprising. On May 5 Charles IV ceded to Napoleon the rights of the Bourbons to the throne of Spain, while Ferdinand accepted a pension and the offer of a residence at Valençay. Napoleon enthroned his brother Joseph and announced his intention of giving Spain a new, reformed constitution. But it was too late ; the tragic incidents at Madrid had infuriated every patriotic Spaniard and all eastern Spain and Andalusia were ablaze. When Joseph entered his capital, every window was shut, nobody in the streets ; it was like a city of the dead. Some days later 7000 French troops, cut off by 25000 Andalusians, surrendered. But now Napoleon came on the scene and in a whirlwind campaign he conquered the whole peninsula, right down to Cadiz.

All Goya's friends, men of learning, intellectuals and enlightened members of the aristocracy, were in favour of the new, liberal ideas for which France stood and most of them were willing to co-operate with the new monarch. Joseph, a scrupulous, rather shy man, genuinely loved Spain and asked for nothing better than to govern her by the Spanish, for the Spanish. And very soon the old feudal rights were suppressed, likewise the Inquisition, while two thirds of the convents were closed and a new constitution proclaimed. But even the best reforms, when imposed by a foreign power, are of no avail. To a man the Spaniards rose in defence of a régime they had detested and against which, once it was re-instated by their efforts, they made haste to rebel.

Goya knew too much about human nature to be blind to the cruel paradox of the political situation, and he identified himself too closely with the Spanish people not to share its natural resentments. But he was clear-sighted enough to foresee the personal risks he was incurring. Moreover he could not subscribe without reserve to the doctrines of any party ; he was no less appalled by the sufferings of his compatriots than by their political obtuseness ; and he had no illusions as to what the future had in store. Throughout these

FRANCISCO GOYA (1746-1828). THE POWDER GRINDERS, CA. 1812. DETAIL.
PALACE OF THE ESCORIAL.

97

FRANCISCO GOYA (1746-1828). THE SHOOTINGS OF MAY THIRD, 1808, AT MADRID (1814). DETAIL.
PRADO, MADRID.

FRANCISCO GOYA (1746-1828). CHRIST IN THE GARDEN OF OLIVES, 1819. (18½ × 13¾″)
CHURCH OF SAN ANTON, MADRID.

years of ordeal his ready sympathy for human suffering never faltered, he never played false to his natural impulses. Thus his changes of front need not be attributed to sordid or selfish motives. In 1808, in pursuance of his official duties, he painted the portrait of the new king Ferdinand VII. He witnessed the street fighting of May 2. We may well imagine how the heroic resistance of Saragossa stirred the heart of the staunch old Aragonese that Goya was; invited by General Palafox (in August) to view the glorious ruins of the city and paint the portraits of the leaders of the resistance, he made haste to respond to the call. He could hardly recognize the city where he had spent his boyhood. The sketches he made, with tears in his eyes, are lost for ever; some months later when the city was captured after a second siege, the French officers slashed them to pieces with their swords, in Palafox's billet. Goya fled to Fuendetodos, his birthplace, and stayed there, sickened by the horrors he had been forced to witness; thus he was able to absent himself from Madrid on March 1, 1809, and escape having to swear allegiance to King Joseph whose rule had now begun.

The French were now in the saddle. Goya returned to his house, his mind haunted by the atrocities of the recent war and its toll of human folly. He resumed his post of Court Painter under the new monarch, but he had little heart for work. He was, however, forced to perform the distasteful task of selecting, with two colleagues, fifty pictures by Spanish artists for despatch to Napoleon's Art Museum — but it would seem that he took care to chose inferior works. In February, 1810, he painted the *Allegory of the City of Madrid* in which, borne by angels, is a medallion showing in profile the head of " *el rey intruso* " copied, as Goya had not yet seen the King, from an engraving. (Later, this effigy was erased and replaced by the words *Dos de Mayo*.) He painted Manuel Romero, Minister of Home Affairs, and other " *afrancesados*," amongst them Canon Juan Antonio Llorente, ex-secretary and historian of the Inquisition, a clever, broad-minded man and an old friend of the artist, who some years later was to meet him again in exile at Bordeaux. On June 15 he attended a special session of the Academy in honor of the Marquis of Almanara who had been appointed ' Protector ' by King Joseph. Finally, on March 18, 1811, he accepted the decoration of the Order of Spain (contemptuously named by patriots " the Order of the Eggplant " owing to the color of the ribbon); it is proved, however, that he never wore it. He also painted some portraits for his private satisfaction: of his friend Goicoechea and his grandson Marianito (born in 1808). On June 3, 1811, he made his will and his wife did likewise; she died in 1812. In this connection a list of his pictures was drawn up; it included *The Colossus* and *Majas on a Balcony*.

In 1812 the wheel turned full circle. Wellington made his triumphal entry into Madrid in August of that year, and Goya painted him on horseback. Though he had no illusions about the men and the organizations that were now exploiting the turn of events in their own interests, or about the *soi-disant* élite who were excitedly retrieving their titles, wealth and privileges from the wagon-trains of the foreigner, he was not blind to the glamour of those local heroes who were springing into prominence all over Spain — men like Empecinado, the daredevil leader of the *guerilleros* of Castile, who was sent to prison for his pains and ended his days as a common criminal. Goya painted his portrait and also announced his intention of " immortalizing with his brush the most heroic exploits of our glorious uprising against the tyrant of Europe." In pursuance of this program he made his equestrian portrait of General Palafox, a work done to order and not as used to be thought (by reason of his trip to Saragossa in 1808) on the battle-front; its date is 1814. It was now that he painted his two masterpieces: *May Second at the Puerta del Sol* and *The Shootings of May Third*. These two great pictures, painted six years after the events depicted, are full of violent movement and the most vivid realism; however it is clear that Goya painted them less from memories of what he had seen than as syntheses of all the incidents whose horror had impressed him and of which his etchings *The Disasters of War* are so scathing an indictment. (These etchings, whose target was not only the misdeeds of the French soldiery but war in general, were not made public during Goya's lifetime — another proof of his divided purposes.)

In these two world-renowned pictures Goya stepped up his colors to an almost frenzied intensity by the use of sudden bursts of light, and those famous greenish glints on the white horse illustrate the boldness of his new technique. That unforgettable figure of the man with outstretched arms (in the *Shootings*), who is gazing wild-eyed at the firing squad with a look of mingled terror and defiance, is the most grandiose tribute to the anonymous heroism of a nation fighting for its independence that the world has seen.

FRANCISCO GOYA (1746-1828). THE COLOSSUS, OR PANIC, CA. 1808. (45½ × 41¼″)
PRADO, MADRID.

FRANCISCO GOYA (1746-1828). FANTASTIC VISION, 1819-1823. (48½×104″)
PRADO, MADRID.

King Ferdinand returned to Madrid on March 24, 1814. He is said to have severely lectured Goya before confirming him in his post, telling him he deserved to be hanged but as a great artist would be forgiven. The return of this fatuous monarch in the guise of a conquering hero was nothing short of grotesque. Three years before, the Cortes of Cadiz, supreme expression of Spanish patriotism struggling against the foreign yoke, had announced that they were fighting in the cause of liberty and the true ideals of the French Revolution, and had drawn up a reformed constitution based on that of King Joseph. Ferdinand's first act was to put this document in his pocket, send the deputies packing, and re-establish an autocratic, inquisitorial régime. It would seem that Goya had reasons to fear the 'purges' that were now the order of the day. An obituary of the Aragonese Canon José Duaso y Latre mentions that the Canon sheltered Goya for three months during this period of personal danger. Count de la Viñaza, who discovered this document, thinks it applies to the year 1814, but Sanchez Canton suggests that it refers more probably to 1823, the year when Ferdinand, with the backing of French Royalist troops, was making another drive against the Liberals. (This also would account for Goya's departure to Bordeaux.) However Nuñez de Arenas in his excellent *Goya's Life in France* prefers to revert to the earlier date, 1814, pointing out that in the years preceding 1823 Goya had kept completely clear of politics, nor had he any relations with the liberal régime that was overthrown ; whereas in 1814 his attitude towards the French during the occupation must have seemed suspicious, to say the least of it, to the monarchists. It was Duaso, then highly esteemed by all parties, who tided his compatriot over this anxious period.

After undergoing trial by a special 'purge' court, Goya resumed his official duties, though he had little heart for them. He painted some large ceremonial portraits of the King for Santander, Saragossa and other cities. As usual, he showed no indulgence to his model ; as a sitter, the Duke of San Carlos, First Chamberlain, inspired him more, and this was the last of his official works to have any *brio*. He also painted the Duchess of Abrantes and the young Duke of Osuna, but he preferred having his friends, Rafael Esteve the engraver, Manuel Garcia, Ramon Satue, Tiburcio Perez the architect and Asensio Julio, a pupil of his and his assistant, sit for him. Despite his official functions Goya seldom visited the Palace. His last big work was his *Junta of the Philippines*, now the pride of the Museum of Castres, a group portrait showing Ferdinand presiding at a session of the 'Council of the Philippines ' or perhaps as some think a meeting of the five Merchants' Guilds at

Madrid. The disproportion between the hugeness of the setting and the smallness of the figures is such as to dwarf the ostensible theme. Obviously it was the rendering of space that interested Goya here and the vast tracts of emptiness are strewn with spots of light and enigmatic forms, while the figures are mere accessories.

In February 1819 Goya bought a country villa, surrounded by large grounds, just outside Madrid on the far side of the Manzanares, beyond the Segovia Bridge, and settled there with Doña Leocadia Zorilla, a relative of his, who had been married to a German named Weiss. On the walls he gave visible form to the specters of his imagination, his personal mythology. His neighbors were intrigued by the presence of the famous artist in their midst and always spoke of the house as the " *Quinta del Sordo*." This strange retreat, on which he left the indelible imprint of his genius, was evidently the scene of curious comings and goings; an inventory revealed the presence of a surprising number of chairs, which seems to indicate that he had many visitors. But most intriguing of all is that eerie world into which we are so dramatically plunged the moment we cross the threshold of this world-famous house which was Goya's home for so many years.

A large room on the ground floor served as dining-room and living-room. On either side of the doorway were painted the following scenes: the *Manola*, showing a woman dressed a a 'Maja' leaning on a big rock, and the *Old Brother*, a bearded ancient propped on his stick while a friend yells some evil message into his deaf ear. Facing these are *Saturn devouring one of his Children* and *Judith and Holophernes*. On the side walls are two large scenes facing each other: the *Pilgrimage of San Isidro* and the *Aquelarre* or *Witches' Sabbath*. These works are so to speak a summing-up of the ideas which had been simmering in Goya's mind for years, his memories and favorite themes ; but never had he bodied forth these phantom

FRANCISCO GOYA (1746-

He painted these directly on the walls, in oils, with a curiously restricted palette: black, white, burnt Siena and Castile earth—colors, that is to say, coming from the earth itself. He began by depicting the most typical figures of his repertory : gluttonous old men, shameless old hags, wily priests, alluring courtesans—monstrous, life-size incarnations of those anomalies of the human situation which he illustrated so copiously in his 'Caprices' and 'Follies.' Though some of the figures are incredibly fantastic, we usually find details linking them up with contemporary realities. (Always interested in out-of-the-way events or quasi-scientific fancies, Goya painted balloon ascents, the wreck of the 'Medusa' and even flying men.) Thus we see a soldier pointing his gun at people sitting in the air above him, and sexless Parcae brandishing ridiculous 'attributes' above the tree-tops. Other pictures are easier to interpret ; that for instance of two men stuck knee-deep in a quagmire belaboring each other with sticks, unable to advance or to retreat ; or, again, that dog's head on the margin of a landscape desolate to the point of evanescence, obviously an emblem of utter loneliness ; or, yet again, the picture of Saturn devouring his children, a symbol almost repellent in its brutal lucidity.

Spain was still seething with political unrest, but Goya no longer played any part in the vicissitudes of his country. His friends, however, joined in setting up a reformed liberal constitution, soon to be overthrown by the French troops Ferdinand called in to the rescue. Apparently Goya was not affected by the repressive measures which followed, forcing many Spaniards into exile. But Doña Leocadia, who had strong views (she seems to have shared in the political activities of the Spanish Freemasons) and made no secret of her loathing for the government in power, was obliged in 1823 to move to Bordeaux with her son Guillermo and daughter Rosario, a child of ten who was Goya's godchild and on whom he doted. Probably Goya, who did not get on well with his son, missed their companionship and this was one of the reasons why he applied for some months' leave to take the waters at Plombières, in France. He was not only given leave but allowed to retain his official post and salary—which shows that the political motives behind his departure were unsuspected. Actually he had been contemplating this move for some time and had no intention of returning; as early as September 17, 1823, he had made over the Quinta del Sordo to his grandson Mariano.

Goya crossed the frontier in June, 1824, and, despite the pretext for his leave, began by stopping some days in Bordeaux, where his friend Moratin was living in exile. " He looked terribly old and weak," Moratin tells us, " and not knowing a word of French felt rather lost. All the same he was delighted to be in France and eager to see everything and everyone." After staying three days in a pension kept by Manuel Silvela, he went to Paris, arriving on June 30, and took lodgings at 5, rue Marivaux.

Nuñez de Arenas has published some interesting extracts from the police records regarding Goya's stay in Paris. The day before his arrival the Ministry of the Interior passed orders that the old painter was to be kept under discreet surveillance with a view to making sure that he was not having any contacts which " in view of his being employed by the Spanish Court might be undesirable." The police reported that Goya had no visitors and owing to his difficulty in speaking French and hardness of hearing, he mostly stayed at home, going out only to see the monuments and take the air. " He looks even older than his years, and moreover is extremely deaf."

It would be pleasant to be able to record that during his two months in Paris Goya met the contemporary French artists, in particular young Delacroix who already knew the Caprichos (which obviously inspired some of his sketches) and had seen the portrait of Guillemardet. Actually, however, it seems that the old painter visited only his compatriots, amongst them Joaquin Ferrer, José Maria Cardano (who had been manager of the first lithographic printing works in Madrid) and Gonzalez Arnao, at whose home the Countess of Chinchon and the Marchioness of Pontejos—who had sat for Goya's most brilliant portraits a quarter of a century before—were often to be seen. Anyhow we may safely assume that Goya visited the Louvre, where the pictures were grouped in three sections, the French, Dutch and Italian Schools (Spanish works being included in the last-named group), and of his private dream-world with such startlingly savage violence. Thus in the *Pilgrimage* we see massed round the guitarist (whose white eyes recall the blind guitarist of the tapestry cartoon) not a mere conventional group of pilgrims but a pyramid of singing faces, whose queer triangular distortion seems the visual embodiment of one tremendous cry. Similarly all the previous scenes of witchcraft are synthesized in the *Aquelarre*, though compared with it they seem innocuous poetic fancies. Here we have an accumulation of all the world's ugliness, every physical and moral degradation, the ravages of age, life's cruelties and madness, presided over by the black Satanic he-goat, immovable as a rock, ineluctable as evil. Above the misshapen bodies and ungainly limbs the mass of faces reminds us of a dark sea pitted with staring eyes. This world of creatures of the night is a ghastly parody of the Creation.

A room of the same size on the floor above was Goya's study. The paintings were disposed in the same way as on the ground floor except that, because of the windows, there were two scenes on each side wall. Beside the door was the *Dog buried in the Sand* with, as a pendant to it, a scene which soon went to pieces and has disappeared. (Possibly the isolated panel of *The Old Woman eating her Soup* was here originally, but it is generally supposed to have been above a door.) Facing the *Dog* are *Two Women laughing at a Man* and *The Reading* in which five men are drinking in the words of a man who is reading to them. On one side wall are *The Parcae* and *The Fight*; on the other the *Pilgrimage to the Fountain of San Isidro*, a grotesquely attired group like a cortege of the forces of the past, and the *Fantastic Vision*. In the latter clearly defined buildings, perched on a crag shaped like the base of a pillar, rise in a landscape background. Here we have a theme that always haunted Goya's imagination, that of 'escape,' escape to an ideal city accessible only by air and a flight beset with deadly perils.

1828). WITCHES' SABBATH, 1819-1823. (55 × 172″) PRADO, MADRID.

FRANCISCO GOYA (1746-1828). THE PILGRIMAGE OF SAN ISIDRO, 1819-1823. DETAIL.
PRADO, MADRID.

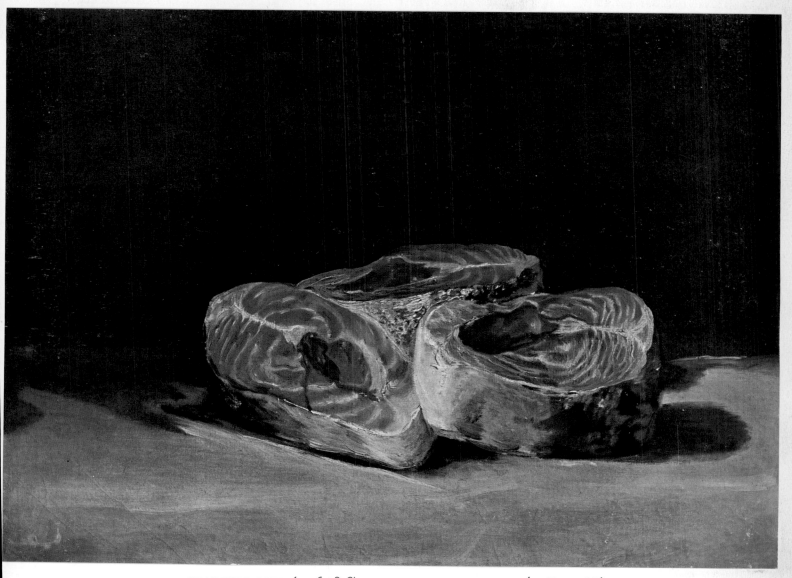

FRANCISCO GOYA (1746-1828). STILL LIFE WITH SALMON. (17½×24¼″)
OSKAR REINHART COLLECTION, WINTERTHUR.

likewise the Luxembourg where David now reigned triumphant and to which the earliest works of Delacroix and Ingres had won admission. Goya may have found time, too, to visit the Salon which opened a few days before he left and to see those epoch-making pictures: Constable's *Hay-Wain, Hampstead Heath* and *The Lock*, Delacroix's *Massacre of Scio* and *Young Girl in a Graveyard*.

After his Paris trip Goya returned to Bordeaux, the city where most of his friends were living and which acted as a link between Spain and the outside world. The Spaniards residing there met daily and indulged in those endless confabulations, hopeful or nostalgic, which are the solace of the exile, their meeting-place being a room (dignified by the name of " the Lions' Den ") in the house of Braulio Poc, one of the heroic defenders of Saragossa. Goya was the bright, particular star at these gatherings ; he was plied with questions about his past, spoke freely and aired his views. Thus the ' legend ' took form on which his first biographers, Matheron and Yriarte, were to draw to good effect. There were men of high intelligence and much political acumen among the refugees, but none had such vitality, enthusiasm and creative energy as the old artist, now almost in his eighties. His fits of rage, ungovernable passions and restless activity were the talk and the wonder of the little group, and his interest in the oddities of visual experience was as keen as ever. He spent much time at fairs and circuses, where he never tired of watching the acrobats, animals and freaks doing their turns. He continued painting, drawing, etching, and learnt the technique of lithography, then in its beginnings. His mind had lost nothing of its alertness ; one of his sketches, depicting an old man, bears the inscription " I'm still learning." Doña Leocadia looked after him and accompanied him everywhere (the story goes that it was she who was so fond of circuses and freaks) ; a somewhat domineering and bustling woman, she had a mania for moving house, but her devoted care for Goya was above all praise. Little Rosario was the apple of his eye, and Goya observed with delighted wonder her childish grace, her vivacity, her precocious talent for drawing and painting.

In the spring of 1826 Goya decided he must set his affairs in order ; also he wished to arrange for an extension of his leave, so as to go on drawing his salary. Against the advice of his friends he went to Madrid, traveling alone. He was given no trouble of any kind, stayed with his son and spent his days revisiting old friends and the haunts of his youth. He had no difficulties at all with the authorities; the King went so far as to honor him by ordering his successor to paint his portrait " for the benefit of posterity."

Returning to Bordeaux, his mind at rest, he resumed his wonted activities. In 1827, at the age of 81, he painted the portrait of Don Juan Bautisto Muguiro and *The Milk-Woman of Bordeaux* ; the technique of tiny brushstrokes here employed forestalled that of the Impressionists. Indeed, as Sanchez Canton writes, he had a " presentiment " of modern painting. His last work, left unfinished, the portrait of José Pio de Molina, a former liberal mayor of Madrid (Reinhart Collection, Switzerland), is also a remarkable anticipation of the future.

In March, 1828, feeling ill, he took to his bed. His daughter-in-law and grandson on their way to Paris stopped at Bordeaux and, feeling better, he got up to receive them. On April 1 he again felt unwell and had to go back to bed. Writing in bed he added as a postscript to a letter Mariano was sending his father, the following words, his testament : *My dear Javier, All I want to tell you is that all this joy has been too much for me, I am feeling out of sorts and am now in bed. May God grant that you come to fetch them, and then my cup of happiness will be full. Good-bye. Your father, Francisco.*

Next morning he awoke half paralysed. Thirteen days later on April 16, 1828, he died, unable to speak but in full possession of his wits. He was buried at Bordeaux, and there were many visitors to his grave, in which his old friend Goicoechea had already been laid to rest. When the grave was opened at the end of the century, it was impossible to distinguish between the two bodies and it was discovered that the head of one was missing. A picture by a painter named Fierros purporting to represent Goya's skull obtained a somewhat gruesome notoriety at the time. The mingled ashes of the two friends now repose in the hermitage of San Antonio de la Florida, beneath the lovely, sensual young women with angels' wings of Goya's fresco.

Every great artist builds up a world of his own, his secret kingdom. Goya's had two aspects, complementary like light and darkness, the real and the imaginary ; each is indispensable to, and impinges on the other, often in surprising ways. Spain is *par excellence* a land of contrasts, a land where faith thrives on sacrilege, life on gambling with death, virtue on contacts with vice, and Goya was well aware of the value of these contrasts to the artist ; indeed they supply as it were the background, lacking which there is no perspective. Baudelaire admired Goya's art of making the monstrous seem so real. This he could do because for him the monstrous was not a mere whimsy but a primordial aspect of reality. " The Slumber of the Mind breeds Monsters " is the legend on one of his most famous etchings. Actually, all that is needed is for the imagination to borrow from the reasoning mind its lucidity ; life can be relied on to demonstrate the seemingly most far-fetched horrors that exist beneath the placid surface of the world. " Events speak " — and Goya was telling only the bitter truth when he wrote : " I saw it, and this tells it."

Those tragic events of which he was an eyewitness evoked strange after-images in his mind's eye, and he interpreted their secret meaning. Indeed the message of his most personal works — the etchings and, above all, the paintings in " The Deaf Man's House " — is nothing short of a philosophy : a philosophy of the absurd, and of despair. In these, during the darkest hours of his cloistered life, he faced up to the scheme of things, interrogated destiny, and himself supplied the answers.

Thus, going beyond the scenes of horror he depicted, hospitals, madhouses, acts of cannibalism, tortures, he penetrated to the heart of that which gives rise to them : a sort of Baroque fatality governing all men and all things, whose outward symbol is the bullfight. And, going yet a stage further with his *Disparates*, pictures of madmen's ballets, showers of animals, landscapes whose skies are cluttered with weird creatures, he forced his way behind the veil of appearance to the latent mechanism of the scheme of things.

FRANCISCO GOYA (1746-1828). THE MILK-WOMAN OF BORDEAUX, 1827. (29 × 26½")
PRADO, MADRID.

NEOCLASSICISM AND ROMANTICISM

Goya was not a precocious genius. His early work for the tapestry-factory merely formed part of a joint enterprise in which several other painters collaborated. Some of the best of the portraits produced at this time are signed by Inza, Carnicero and Esteve, though, if unsigned, they are sometimes attributed to Goya. In his exhaustive study of the *Antecedents, Coincidences and Influences of Goya's Art* Enrique Lafuente Ferrari has carefully sorted out these attributions, analysing the personal characteristics of each painter and giving each his due. Goya never accepted pupils in his studio; he was far too much of an individualist to care for teaching and, in any case, when his success might have led him to consider doing so, his infirmity precluded it. Thus in 1795 he felt obliged to decline the post of President of the Academy of Painting on the grounds of his total deafness. Still as regards Esteve, we might employ the word that figures in the title of Ferrari's book and speak of a " coincidence. " For a short while the two artists worked side by side. Goya had no taste for making the numerous replicas of his official portraits solicited by various institutions and the Court of the Two Sicilies. Esteve took charge of these with great success (confirmed by Goya's correspondence and in a letter written by Queen Maria Luisa), and by dint of copying he assimilated what has been styled Goya's " grey manner. " This he turned to good account in his original work, which includes some excellent portraits of women and children, notably one of the Duchess of Alba. His color has a glossy, enamel-like finish, and this smoothness of texture, without any loading of the pigment cr roughening of the surface, differentiates his work from Goya's, and he obviously lacks Goya's power of evoking atmosphere.

As the years passed, Goya constantly deepened and renovated his art, always in terms of an inner, purely personal compulsion; thus those who otherwise might have kept in step with him were soon hopelessly outdistanced. This was the case with Esteve whose work after 1800 lost all real resemblance to Goya's, though his career lasted another twenty years. At this time, however, some younger artists were associated with Goya: Ribelles and Ranz intermittently, and Ascensio Julia in a more regular way. Julia was Goya's assistant and worked under his orders on several occasions during the War of Independence. His work is remarkable for the ' short cuts ' in his technique; he used pure, unbroken color applied in flat patches, almost without any graphic delineation — a sort of anticipation of the methods of the Macchiaioli. As time went on, Goya grew ever more ' eccentric,' with the result that a great deal of his work seemed quite incomprehensible to his contemporaries. Thus a reaction set in against it, to which the old artist's self-imposed isolation certainly contributed.

Though on his return from exile Ferdinand VII confirmed Goya in his post, he took into his service some new men, to begin with Vicente Lopez, in whom the King had an artist after his own heart, obsequious and highly competent; and, later, José de Madrazo. Thus the Academy, both ancient and modern, had its revenge, since Lopez was an ideal exponent of the XVIIIth-century style of official painting, while Madrazo, who after staying in Rome and Paris was eager to put into practice the theories of Winckelmann and Mengs and to follow in David's footsteps, stood for the neoclassicism then in the ascendant. Star pupil of the Academy of Valencia, then of Maella at Madrid, Lopez was an accomplished draftsman and technician. His work had caught the eye of Charles IV when he visited Valencia and the King promptly attached him to the Court. In this connection is not some rehabilitation of that hapless monarch's reputation overdue ? Weak and blundering though he may have been politically speaking, he proved himself a true friend of the arts, enlightened to the point of boldness, as is shown not only by his unfailing admiration for so exceptional an artist as Goya but also by his almost excessive eagerness to unearth new talent. In after life, when he had retired to Rome (where he still kept up a small court), it was he again who gave encouragement to the first neoclassical Spanish painters, then regarded as an audacious vanguard. After 1814 Lopez cut a leading figure in Spanish art, as supervisor of the art schools, drawing teacher to Ferdinand's successive wives and official portraitist to the King and his circle. To his prolific brush we owe a unique pictorial record of the outer aspects of

Spanish officialdom during this period; a pageant of statesmen, prelates, judges, academicians and all the hierarchy of a court that, though still in the grip of a punctilious etiquette, was tending by the force of circumstances towards a certain freedom. While his skill in depicting costumes, decorations, ornaments is prodigious, he shows little concern for the psychology of his sitters. In fact his models are always so to speak ' on show,' and their attitudes are tediously stereotyped. In short, this painter of a ' Restoration ' was a man of the old régime.

José de Madrazo, on the other hand, aspired to being a reformer. He was in Paris in 1801, with his friends Juan Aparicio and Juan Antonio Ribera, and studied under David, then at the height of his fame as an art-teacher; after that he went to Rome, at the same time as Ingres. While in Rome during the War of Independence he fell foul of Napoleon's secret agents owing to his avowed loyalty to the Bourbons. On his return to Madrid he was enthusiastically welcomed and promptly set on foot a drastic reform of the academic methods of teaching art. He insisted on classical composition, on drawing from plaster casts of antique statuary, on the cultivation of the Grand Style. He was placed in charge of the organization of the Prado, founded by Ferdinand VII at the suggestion of his second wife and stocked with pictures from the royal collections; he also directed the Royal Institute of Lithography. In short he became dictator of the art world of Madrid, and this dictatorship was carried on for the best part of the century by other artist members of his family. Amongst his sons were an art critic, an architect and some painters; one of them, Federico de Madrazo, a leading portrait-painter during the reign of Isabella, became director of the Prado and the Academy, and had Fortuny for his son-in-law.

Leaving aside Goya's amazing anticipations of the future, which for a long while after his death met with no response in Spain, we find that throughout the XIXth century, owing perhaps to this unawareness of the true national values of Spanish art, there was a curious time-lag between Spanish and French painting. Thus when José de Madrazo set out to play the part of a Spanish David, this was twenty years too late; he was a contemporary of Ingres. Federico de Madrazo, who had been Ingres' pupil, showed himself in his best portraits a worthy disciple of the Frenchman. There is the same time-lag between Delacroix' sketches and the Spanish romantic little masters; as also, later, between Meissonier and Fortuny. And the Catalan and Asturian painters caught up with Impressionism only when Neo-Impressionism had arrived. And so it was all along the line—until the coming of Picasso.

When in Rome, the Madrazos had also been in touch with the ' Nazarenes,' led by Overbeck, who were all for a return to the Primitives. Federico de Madrazo's Ingresque style had a vein of severe Purism stemming from Raphael and Perugino. A Nazarene group established itself at Barcelona where it flourished for many years, its leading figures being Espalter and Clavé. With Juan Aparicio pointing the way, the Academy now made a rapid swerve towards historical painting, so as to align itself with the Romanticism then coming into vogue. Also, it was obvious that themes exploiting the patriotic motive would have a wider appeal than laborious, archaeological reconstitutions of the remote past. Throughout the century the historical subject reigned supreme; it supplied the themes for competitions, was regarded as the touchstone of artistic ability, and the more it abounded in clichés and cheap effects, the greater was its popularity. Beginning with the barbarian invasions, these subjects ranged over the whole field of history, century by century, with special emphasis on the Reconquest and dramatic episodes in the lives of Joanna the Mad, Philip II and the Emperor Charles V, to conclude with the civil wars and the contemporary Moroccan campaigns. But the soaring imagination of a Delacroix, triumphant over time, would have been needed to overcome the discrepancy between these great historic occasions and the banality of the living models used by the artists to incarnate those who took part in them. They could only serve for picturesque details, and thus the artist tended to scale down memorable events to their most trivial, most prosaically anecdotal elements. And the hugeness of these canvases, cluttered up with details, far from remedying these defects, brought them into prominence.

It would be needless to linger on the circumstances which led historical painting in Spain as in so many other countries to degenerate into the anecdotal or into a vapid ' social realism ,' were it not that one genuinely original painter sought to arrest this gradual decline. This was Eduardo Rosales, who no less by his early training and associations than by the fact of his taking part in the great national and international competitions of the day, by his choice of subjects and the rules he imposed on himself, seemed marked out to be an exponent of academic painting at its most traditional. Nevertheless he cuts the figure of a belated romantic (he was consumptive and his career had the meteoric brevity of Chopin's) and his sketches prove that he had intimations of better things. In his large canvases, we find simplicity of composition, a feeling for volume, firmness and boldness of design. His colors, however, were always conventional and tame and the whole conception of this art is disputable. When we compare the finished version of his *Testament of Isabella the Catholic*, by general consent his masterwork, with the series of wholly admirable preliminary sketches he made for it, we cannot fail to see how the initial concept has progressively deteriorated. In carefully delineating features and meticulously localizing setting and costumes, Rosales frittered away the creative zest of his first inspiration; the theme is submerged by its development. The very ability of this painter brings out all the more clearly the inherent defects of the principles to which he felt it his duty to adhere. The excellence of the sketches he made during his stay in Murcia, especially those shortly before his death, in which he gives us only the essentials, rendered in sweeping brushstrokes dipped in light, makes us keenly regret his inhibitions.

All the more keenly because, alongside official art, the century witnessed some attempts by individual artists to blaze new trails. The lonely rebel's consolation for the incomprehension of a hostile world is his sense of freedom. Though to begin with, the Spanish romantics profited little by the lesson of freedom they could have learnt from Goya, they were alive to the contemporary spiritual unrest, the social upheaval taking place in Spain and the renascence of truly national values. Their first discovery was that of the natural beauty of their own country. To the French or English traveler Spain, with its colorful cities, its picturesque farrago of survivals from the Middle Ages and the East, the exoticism of its costumes and manners, seems the ideal setting for a romantic's dream. It is essentially a land of contrasts, of violence and passions. And Spanish artists now were becoming aware of this. Thus at Seville a whole school of painters took to making small pictures of the ancient and modern buildings of the city and the people in its streets. At once realistic and imaginative, naïve and unpretentious were the two Becquer brothers, Joaquin and José, the latter of whom was the father of the painter Valeriano Becquer and that great elegiac poet Gustavo Adolfo Becquer. And before long painters in other provinces of Spain began to follow the lead given by the Andalusian artists.

But the master of the genre is Jenaro Perez Villamil (born at El Ferrol in 1807) who on his return from a journey to Porto Rico met the English landscape-painter David Roberts (who stayed two years in Spain, 1832-1833). This meeting was the turning-point in his career. He took over from Roberts the English methods of treating light and the habit of open-air painting. Villamil specialized in ruins, castles and mediaeval cathedrals, stressing their more fantastic aspects, mixed with the romantic writers of the day, indulged in foreign travel (developing a marked enthusiasm for the ancient buildings in Flanders) and brought out a series of *Picturesque Views of Spain*, lithographed in Paris after his sketches. He also traveled in Italy and the Near East and, while building up a copious *œuvre* (8000 pictures and 18,000 watercolors and sketches), also found time to teach landscape at the Academy. His successor to this post, after his death, was Francisco Ferrant, a painter of nightscapes inspired by the German landscapists.

From the War of Independence, the clash between new ideas and ancient institutions and the necessity for every Spaniard of taking sides, a new type of man had emerged—a man with a sense of responsibility, of human dignity, of individual values. Amongst the first generation of Romantics, men who were spurred on to greater efforts by the opposition they encountered, were two excellent painters who incarnated the spirit of the movement: José Esquivel and Leonardo Alenza. Contemporaries of Villamil, they were born in 1806 and

1807 respectively. Esquivel was a Sevillian (his father was killed in the Battle of Bailen) and he studied in the School of Fine Arts of his native city, whose students were still copying Murillo. He had struck out for himself with scenes of Andalusian life before he went to Madrid in 1831 with his friend José Gutierrez de la Vega, who was soon to make his name as a society portrait-painter as well as being a commendable painter of religious subjects. The romantic movement was well under way and Esquivel hastened to join the 'Liceo Artistico y Literario,' a group that actively promoted the new ideas, ran a review of its own and organized exhibitions and literary gatherings. It was thanks to the opportune help of this group that when suddenly stricken with blindness he was able to keep afloat. After his sight was restored almost miraculously (he had made two attempts at suicide), he continued painting in various genres, and also wrote critical articles and drew up plans for new methods of teaching art. His best works are portraits of his friends: writers, artists, actors, liberal politicians. He was a bosom friend of the poet José Zorilla who had made a name for himself with his miscellanies of the national legends. Esquivel shows him reading his poems to a group of writers, and their portraits are remarkably true to life. He also had a gift for rendering an atmosphere of domesticity, and though for the most part we do not even know the names of the sitters for the innumerable portraits he turned out, they give collectively a vivid impression of the life of a quiet, well-mannered middle class, too discreet to indulge in any show of personal emotion. True, the poses are somewhat hackneyed, there is nothing particularly interesting in the setting, and the costumes are uniformly dark and drab ; nevertheless the merits of these portraits of worthy, eminently likeable people, people one could trust, are undeniable.

The work of Leonardo Alenza, who died young, at the age of thirty-eight, if shrewder and subtler, moved within a narrower range. He had exceptional gifts of observation and improvisation ; indeed this quick-witted, keen-eyed young Madrilenian was the best painter of the everyday life of his age. With a strict economy of means and a fine sense of balanced lay-out, he depicts street scenes, picturesque groups and individuals, and cafés. A born illustrator, he did much excellent work for the reviews of the day and indeed the most striking part of his *œuvre* consists in his drawings, now in the National Library, Madrid. His most famous picture, a view of the interior of the Café de Levante, has perished, but we can realize how good it was from the preliminary sketch. The small pictures in the Museum of Romantic Art, Madrid, are witty mockeries of the romantic affectations of the day, notably the cult of suicide. It was probably this gift for satire and fantasy that led a contemporary to write on the occasion of his death (in 1845) that with him died " the last memory of Goya."

GOYA'S IMITATORS

It is curious how few recalls of Goya can be detected in the first phase of Spanish romantic art. Not until a second generation (born at the time of Goya's departure from Spain) came on the scene, did his influence make itself widely felt and his genius receive fitting recognition. In 1846 for the first time a ' Homage to Goya ' was the theme of an exhibition (at the *Liceo* in Madrid); thirteen works by him were shown and with them pictures by his friends Julia and Carderera—and even by little Rosario Weiss.

In the middle of the nineteenth century there arose a veritable cult of Goya whose most fervent devotees were two outstanding artists of the new generation: Eugenio Lucas (born 1824) and Federico Lameyer (born 1825). Lameyer, who had worked with Alenza and inherited his gift for illustration, contributed successfully to magazines. A highly expert draftsman, he had a flexibility of style enabling him to align himself with the artists whom he admired, and on him, as on Lucas, Goya's art exercised an irresistible fascination. These two young painters copied Goya's works, drew inspiration from them, and finding in them a vein as yet unexploited, employed his themes, the result being that it is often difficult to distinguish between the elements of imitation and interpretation of the master in their works. Nevertheless it was on a remarkably limited part of Goya's *œuvre* that their interest centered and it was the anecdotal aspect of his pictures that they tried to reproduce: Inquisition scenes, public festivals, masquerades, ' majas,' bullfights, exploits of bandits or smugglers. Their chief sources were the small genre pictures in the Academy of San Fernando, the two series of etchings of *Caprices* and *Bullfights*, and the ' *Bulls of Bordeaux.* '

As regards Eugenio Lucas some eminent contemporary authorities on Spanish art have seen in this artist more than a mere imitator and sought to isolate his real personality. The first step in this direction was to distinguish his works from those of his son of the same name, who persistently used his father's themes but with diminished vigor. The elder Lucas had a genius for sketches dashed off on the spur of the moment; when still quite young (in 1842) he started painting genre scenes and portraits in the manner of Lopez. He was in close touch with the romantic landscape-painters and especially with Villamil, whose sister he married. Such was his technical facility that he turned out his pictures as rapidly as his brother-in-law, and such his gift of assimilation that he could copy Goya, Watteau and Tiepolo no less successfully than the little Dutch masters and even Velazquez. Keenly interested in the events of the day, he painted scenes of the 1854 Revolution, and he was also a great traveler, making frequent trips to North Africa in quest of exotic subject-matter. When in Paris he made the acquaintance of Manet with whom he exchanged a number of letters, which unfortunately have been lost. Caring little for public recognition, he moved outside official circles and his success, considerable though it was, brought him neither profit nor any great renown. Still, this did not prevent his son Eugenio Lucas Villamil, Angel Lizcano and Francisco Domingo Marquès from following in his footsteps for some time. Some of his works after passing through the hands of shady picture-dealers and undergoing various touchings up have been taken for authentic Goyas and found their way into even such famous art museums as those of Munich and Vienna. Indeed few painters have suffered as much as Goya at the hands of forgers, and we must be constantly on our guard against mistaken attributions such as those in A. L. Mayer's Catalog and those of the recent exhibition at Bordeaux. But it would be unjust to saddle the elder Lucas with the blame for these fakes, mostly of a poor order, and his original work may well claim a place in the lineage of Goya's minor productions. Lucas knew his limitations and skillfully masked the lapses in his drawing by conveniently placed shadows or hatchings; he had a sense of rhythm and movement and painted with small, vibrant brushstrokes. Goya's volumes and accents are never present in his work; on the contrary, he seeks to render atmosphere by suggestive arrangements of color like those of the Impressionists.

That for a great part of the XIXth century the true purport of Goya's *œuvre* was not understood even by those who deemed themselves his warmest admirers, need not surprise us. For the understanding of such art a certain lapse of time is needed; thus its early evaluations by Théophile Gautier are far less discerning than those by Baudelaire. Indeed it was not until the advent of Daumier and Manet that his message found an adequate response.

What place should we assign in the history of living art to that master of the small picture, Fortuny ? There is no denying that he was versatile, prodigiously observant and a superb technician, and yet there was a curious superficiality in his attitude to art; not only did he confine himself to rendering the outward aspects of things, but he depreciated as it were the art of those whom he admired. Thus he saw in Goya merely a painter of picturesque scenes of Spanish life. Fascinated by the glamour of the East, this Catalan, who had accompanied the Spanish army in the Moroccan campaign, was always hankering for the light of Africa and found in Granada the place of his heart's desire. As for the revolution in the way of seeing that was taking place in France and even in Italy, it obviously meant nothing to him. Still, the small historical pictures to which he devoted himself so assiduously are excellent of their kind; indeed he breathed new, vivid life into the genre so ponderously exploited by Meissonier. His rise to fame was spectacular; he became wealthy almost overnight and idolized all over Europe. Yet some of his tiny sketches are such exquisite records of fugitive impressions that one wonders if Fortuny was the dupe of his success and if when he died (at the age of thirty-six) he had not in him the makings of a really fine artist.

EXPRESSIONISM AND IMPRESSIONISM

Now that the Romantic painters' attempt to resuscitate values of a genuinely national order had petered out into a merely anecdotal art and a sort of standardized 'Hispanicism,' two courses lay open to the Spanish artists, who by now were well aware of having been outdistanced by the evolution of painting in neighboring countries; they could either exploit the discoveries of the open-air school and paint the Spanish landscape as it really was, or else they could intensify the national characteristics in their art. Many Spanish artists (amongst them Lameyer and Lucas)kept up personal relations with France. The landscapist Martin Rico, a friend of Daubigny, ended by settling in Paris. Actually the artist who did most to introduce the realistic landscape into Spain was a Belgian, Carlos Haes (born at Brussels in 1829 and educated at Malaga where his father had settled). After completing his art training in Belgium Haes returned to Spain in 1857 and, having acquired Spanish nationality, succeeded Ferrant in the post of teacher of landscape at the Academy of Madrid, and during his thirty years' tenure of his official post opened the eyes of successive generations of students to the beauties of nature. Amongst his pupils were Beruete, Riancho, Sainz and Regoyos; indeed there were few young artists at Madrid who did not benefit by his instruction. At Barcelona Ramon Marti y Alsina (born in 1826) had a more or less similar influence; he brought a forceful realism to his city views, peopled with colorful crowds. Joaquin Vareyda, who was his most brilliant disciple and excelled in rendering atmosphere with soft, delicately blurred brushstrokes, did most of his work in a particularly beautiful region of the Province of Gerona —whence the name of the " School of Olot " given his followers.

A fine scholar and compiler of the first descriptive catalog of Velazquez' works, Aureliano de Beruete, painted views of the Manzanares, Madrid and Toledo, characterized by their delicate brushwork, subtle color-schemes and harmonies of greys and blues. Agustin Riancho and Casimirio Sainz hailed from the Province of Santander, Diario de Regoyos from Asturia. Cantabrian Spain, with its green fields, soft light and misted skies, has much in common with the countryside of northern France dear to the Impressionists, and is in fact an ideal region for the painter who treats light as his paramount concern. Born in 1857, Regoyos studied at Madrid, made a brief stay in Paris and then migrated to Brussels where he joined the group of writers and artists moving in the orbit of Verhaeren, Rodenbach, Constantin Meunier and Theo van Rysselberghe. He gave his first exhibition at *L'Essor* and was a member of the ' XX ' Club. In 1883 he went to Spain with a group of Belgian artists and in 1888 with Verhaeren, and their enthusiasm for the country found expression in a book named *L'Espagne noire*. While in Paris, Regoyos saw much of Mallarmé, Degas, Redon, Pissarro and Signac. He adopted the procedures of Divisionism but handled them with a flexibility enabling him to retain his spontaneity of expression; indeed, even in exploiting the latest technical discoveries, he kept his spontaneity, for he always wished his landscapes to be, as the saying went, " full of soul." He died at Barcelona in 1913. Though unappreciated in his lifetime, he justly ranks today as one of the greatest modern Spanish painters.

Born in 1863 at Valencia, Joaquin Sorolla, thanks to his prestige and influence, brought to an end the practice of painting in the studio; he employed a very free technique of sweeping brushstrokes resembling that of his friend Zorn. In his pictures of the sea-coast, Sorolla rendered to perfection the white, limpid light flooding the bodies of bathers and the pale sheen of water lapping the sand or the hulls of boats. It is interesting to compare this, the best part of his *œuvre*, with the later developments of the art of Francisco Iturrino, revealed at the epoch-making exhibition in Madrid, which was organized in connection with the first (1951) Hispano-American Biennale by Juan Ramon Masoliber, with a view to determining who were the pioneers in Spain of the modern way of seeing. Iturrino, who was born in 1880 and died in 1924, was undoubtedly influenced by Cézanne and the early phase of the Fauve movement; he gave his first exhibition, along with Picasso, at Vollard's. Using bathers as his themes, he concentrated on arrangements of colors, geometrical to begin with, then freely rhythmic, and he sought to render movement by breaking it up into its elements.

This 1951 Exhibition also did belated justice to two excellent Catalan painters, Francisco Gimeno and Mariano Pidelaserra. Following the atmospheric art of the School of Olot and the descriptive lyricism of Meifren and Mir, a return to more solid form was called for, and this was effected by Gimeno. Born in 1858, he came of a peasant family living at Tortosa, studied under local artists and became a great admirer of Vareyda. Visiting Madrid in 1884, he had no success beyond some encouraging words from Haes. To earn his living he worked as a house-painter, but devoted all his spare time to art. His work is not that of a self-taught or naïve artist but the fruit of earnest, unremitting efforts. Gimeno painted what he had before him, his little home and his large family, and studying the play of light on faces, evolved for himself a sort of facet-painting, stressing planes and volumes. Mariano Pidelaserra, after starting off with a rather tedious realism, showed much ability in meticulously accurate depictions of natural scenes, thickly wooded Catalan hillsides, and in these works his smooth, heavily charged brushstrokes gave place to an austere but vigorous pointillist technique.

From 1890 onward the great city of Barcelona, a prosperous seat of commerce, was plunged into an economic and social crisis. The contrast between the wealth of some and the poverty of others was so glaring that the contemporary anarchist theories of ' direct action ' found a favorable soil. There was a series of outrages, strikes, reprisals, and meanwhile the trade-union movement gathered strength. In 1898, the year of the collapse of the Spanish colonial empire, a crowd of refugees from Cuba poured into the city, and the sudden influx of these unhappy exiles, dependent on public charity, made things even worse. Some young intellectuals and artists, among them Santiago Rusiñol, and Ramon Casas, aesthetes who had been leading the *vie de Bohème* in Paris, turned the situation to account and preached a gospel of revolt against the established order; this certainly contributed to the welcome now accorded to foreign ideas of all kinds. Thus a farrago of conflicting tendencies now invaded the Spanish scene: Pre-Raphaelitism, Maeterlinck's symbolism, Ibsenian ideology, Wagnerian rhapsodizing, Whistlerian languors, and a cult of the seamy side of life, stemming from Steinlen, Forain and even Lautrec. All this was styled " modernism " and though it sometimes lapsed into *fin-de-siècle* decadence, it cleared the ground for such genuine creative achievements as Gaudi's deeply mystical art and the poetic plasticism of Nonell.

Born in 1872 in one of the poor districts of Barcelona, Isidro Nonell died in 1911 in the same city, which he had never left except for some brief trips to Paris, and the uniformity of his life is paralleled by that of his *œuvre*. He always chose what might be called depressing subjects, but this predilection for the lugubrious is redeemed by the splendid integrity of his art. Thus in 1896 he painted the unhappy cretins of the Pyrenean village of Bohi and, thereafter, unprepossessing gipsy hags, emaciated women and enigmatic figures with staring eyes; yet by the perfection of his technique he endowed these queer or pathetic specimens of humanity with real grandeur. In the ' Bohi ' pictures, which were exhibited at Vollard's in 1898 (all of them being sold), Nonell aimed at an angular precision of line, accentuating the dramatic aspects of the subject with a brutality foreshadowing Solana's. But soon he simplified his composition; held together by an overall rhythm, the picture was reduced to a schema of large masses. At this time broken hues of red and green prevailed in Nonell's somber palette; it was only at the close of his life, about 1908, that he took to pure colors and harmonies of pinks and blues.

Nonell is the best Spanish representative of the modern way of seeing and of pure painting. As a result of his early death and that of Regoyos, and Picasso's migration to Paris, Spanish art entered on a period of compromise and caution at the very time when a movement towards a larger freedom was under way abroad, under the leadership, as it so happened, of the Spaniard Picasso. Though in favor of a gradual modernization of traditional methods, Spanish artists were hostile to that movement. The leading figure was Ignazio Zuloaga who stood for the national Spanish values and imposed a new style on renderings of the stock figures of the past—dwarfs, toreros, majas—, while in his justly famous portraits he placed the most representative figures of modern Spain, such as Unamuno and de Falla, against backgrounds in which he sought to synthesize Eternal Spain.

PICASSO

GRIS SOLANA MIRO DALI

During the present century, as a result of widespread changes in the artists' way of seeing and the discovery of new techniques, national frontiers have come to mean less in art. In the great art movements of our time—Cubism, Expressionism, Surrealism—Spanish artists have sometimes played a leading part, whether they made their homes in France or stayed in their own country. Their work, however, belongs to the History of Modern Painting, which has been fully surveyed in previous volumes of this series. Thus in the following pages we shall confine ourselves to briefly recapitulating the chief developments of modern art, with special reference to what they owe to the heritage of Spanish painting and what contributions they have made to it.

PABLO PICASSO (1881). SEATED HARLEQUIN, 1923. (49¼×38″)
OWNED BY MR CHARLES IM OBERSTEG, GENEVA.

PICASSO

PABLO Ruiz Picasso was born at Malaga, October 25, 1881. Like Velazquez and Valdés Leal, the name he made illustrious was that of his mother, Maria Picasso, who came of a family of Majorcan goldsmiths. Her husband was a teacher of drawing (of Basque extraction), José Ruiz Blasco, who when Picasso was born was exercising his profession in Andalusia. Later on, he moved to Corunna and, finally, in 1895 he obtained the much coveted post of professor of drawing at the School of Fine Arts in Barcelona. Thus drawing was so to speak Picasso's first language. So well did he learn its principles and practice that his father allowed him to start painting when he was only ten. He rapidly developed such skill that passing the entrance examination of the Academy of Barcelona was mere child's-play for him; within a few hours he completed the set piece for painting which the candidates were allowed a month. He now began to take part in official competitions and in 1896 went to Madrid, where he passed the entrance examination to the Academy of San Fernando as easily as that of Barcelona. But in Madrid as in Barcelona he had little use for the official curriculum which indeed had nothing to teach him, and much preferred studying the masterpieces in the Prado. Thus he acquired a thorough knowledge of the painting of the past, a knowledge which he broadened by a study of the creative processes behind great works of art, preliminary drawing and sketches, the first versions of the artists' compositional schemes.

But what above all he loved was life itself. He had a prompt affection, at once exacting and undiscriminating, for " things great and small," and a particularly keen interest in the mysterious world of childhood, in the sufferings of the poor and the feverish unrest of city life. In that *fin de siècle* ambiance of the late 'nineties, with its pessimism, its negative values and aesthetic languors, he struck a positive note, such was the vitality of his drawing, the wit and ingenuity of his compositions. On his return to Barcelona in 1897 he was plunged into the great art revival which was by way of making that city a center of European significance and sponsoring the most daring manifestations of a free and vital art. " Modernism " had triumphed some years earlier with the festivals at Sitges in which César Franck's music and Maeterlinck's plays had been revealed to the Spanish public, and which was the scene of a famous procession when two of El Greco's pictures (bought by Santiago Rusiñol) were borne in state to the Museum of Catalan Art. There was in fact a rage for all things modern and what was dubbed in Paris "*l'art nouveau*" flourished exceedingly; floral forms of vaguely oriental inspiration, heraldic devices and a sort of flamboyant Neo-Gothicism were the order of the day. In 1897 one of the moving spirits of the Sitges demonstrations, Pedro Romeu, installed the " Els Quatre Gats " cabaret in a Neo-Gothic building; a Spanish counterpart of the famous " Chat Noir " in Paris, it included a tavern, a restaurant, and a theater for marionettes and galanty-shows, directed by Miguel Utrillo. This was the favorite meeting-place of the young Spanish artists, long-haired and picturesquely attired like their Parisian predecessors. Drawing his inspiration from the spirited, highly effective charcoal drawings of contemporaries and foreign visitors made by Ramon Casas (now to be seen in the Museum of Modern Art in Barcelona), Picasso decorated the walls of the " Quatre Gats " with the portraits of twenty-five artists and writers who frequented it. This, his first public exhibition, won him a notice in *La Vanguardia*. In 1898 he designed a menu card for Romeu, showing the customers sitting at their tables with mugs of beer before them; its lay-out is reminiscent of Japanese prints. By now Picasso's drawing had achieved an individual style; incisive, sometimes tending to caricature, the line is richly expressive. In some of his best works of the period, as in the charcoal drawing of his sister (1899), the composition is enlivened by delicate touches of color. In his contemporary oil painting, Picasso gives the impression of drawing with his brush, and the influence of Casas, more an illustrator than a painter, is still apparent. However, in some other pictures Picasso now began to juxtapose large brushstrokes of more richly worked pigment and to employ broad planes. His range of subjects was much the same as that of Sebastian Junyent, who shared his studio and painted social scenes with a

PABLO PICASSO (1881). CÉLESTINE, 1903. (31¾×23½″)
PRIVATE COLLECTION, PARIS.

PABLO PICASSO (1881). THE SICK CHILD, 1903. (18 × 15 ¾″)
MUSEUM OF MODERN ART, BARCELONA.

sensitive technique like that of Carrière. In 1900 Picasso for the first time had some of his drawings published in Barcelona magazines (*Catalunya artistica* and *Joventut*). In September he went to Paris with his friend Carlos Casagemas.

For a Catalan artist a trip to Paris was then almost obligatory. Rusiñol, Casas and Utrillo lived off and on in Montmartre and kept the Barcelona artists posted as to the latest Parisian developments. For Paris was the Mecca of artists of all nationalities. Picasso's first visit lasted some months, and he stayed in a studio passed on to him by Nonell who had just left. He associated chiefly with Catalan friends, sold a picture with the help of Pere Manach, and returned to Barcelona for Christmas. This trip had a decisive influence on the evolution of his art; not only did he take note on the spot of the themes which Degas, Steinlen and Forain had brought into favor (hitherto known to him only through the intermediacy of Casas), but he closely studied the amazing transpositions of visual experience effected by Lautrec. He sought to interpret this vision on new lines (as had recently been done by Bonnard, Vuillard and the 'Nabis') by more or less divisionist procedures and by the use of patches of increasingly vivid colors and strident contrasts.

For a while his art reflected his nostalgic yearnings for the world he had left, and the pictures he painted in Spain in 1901 were full of reminiscences of Montmartre: street scenes, prostitutes or figures of the Paris underworld, dancers of the Moulin de la Galette, music-hall artists. Yet somehow he imbued these subjects with a Spanish flavor which enlarged their scope, giving them more vigor and more pungency, not to say crudity. In the course of a rapid trip through Andalusia Picasso painted the Spanish dancers in the cabarets of Malaga, wrapped in long shawls like Nonell's gipsies, and now guitars made their first appearance in his art. This was a feverishly active year. In the course of it he went to Madrid to launch the " new style," and with Francisco Soler, the writer, founded a magazine, *Arte Joven*, whose first issue appeared in March, 1901. He was still in close touch with the Barcelona group and this number contained a drawing by Nonell, a message from Ramon Raventos to the intellectuals of Madrid and poems by Verdaguer. In his own contributions Picasso gave free play to his superlative draftsmanship.

The fifth and last number of *Arte Joven* appeared on June 1, when Picasso was back in Barcelona. He left at once for Paris with his friend Junyer-Vidal, a landscapist with a special predilection for Majorca (Picasso made some queer, burlesque portraits of him, echoing his friend's pantheistic handling of landscape). He brought with him to Paris no less than 75 works, which were exhibited on June 24 at the Vollard Galleries in the rue Lafitte along with 36 pictures by the Basque artist Iturrino. Amongst the subjects, besides those *à la Lautrec*, were Spanish scenes, bullfights and horse-races, as well as some nudes and a number of striking flower pieces which so much impressed Félicien Fagus that he wrote at length about them—the first French article to be published on Picasso. This exhibition attracted also the attention of Coquiot (of whom Picasso painted several portraits that year) and won him the friendship of Max Jacob, henceforth his devoted ally in the years of struggle. For Picasso, far from wishing to rest on his laurels, was quite determined not to repeat himself, nor to make concessions, however advantageous it might be.

Indeed it was at Paris that he embraced most fervently those typically Spanish ideals of austerity and abnegation. Abandoning his vehemently expressive Pointillism, he took to using broad, flat planes of white or neutral colors, and blocked out with these his first Pierrots and Harlequins, still rather ungainly and loosely knit as to their form. His next step was to give these masses the definition they had lacked by binding them with thick contour-lines. In his *Women Seated in a Bar* and *Women drinking Absinthe*, the anecdotal element is almost wholly absent; hieratic, doom-fraught figures, stolid lumps of coarse humanity with their elbows pressed to their sides and heavy, rectangular faces, these women incarnate a starkly elemental force. Next Picasso took to using overall rhythms conveying movement, protective, tender, emotive gestures. In his first " *Maternities* " and groups of women and children, we feel his pent-up energy has found a natural outlet and is functioning with a healthy, serene efficacy. In short, the artist's evolution was completed and it is plain to see how vast was the ground covered in that single year, 1901. When Picasso returned to Barcelona early in 1902 he had simplified his way of seeing and created a coherent personal world, the visual embodiment of his philosophy of life.

Fifteen new pictures by Picasso were shown from April 1 to 15 at Berthe Weill's gallery in Paris, the catalog being prefaced by Adrien Farge. But this had not the success of his first exhibition; as was to happen so often in the course of his career, the thought behind his art, its inner logic, met with no response. When Picasso came back to Paris in October, he was very short of money. After living in various lodgings in the Latin Quarter, he moved into Max Jacob's room at the Hôtel Voltaire. His paintings of this period—of circus performers in their motley and blind men and women—are imbued with deeply felt compassion. At the beginning of 1903 Picasso offered all the pictures in his studio for the price of a ticket to Spain, but without success. However he managed to return to Barcelona, where he stayed about a year, and amongst his old friends and in a more understanding *milieu*, he produced the most significant works of his new manner, painting with total freedom and a complete mastery of his means. Even in the commissions he was given, such

PABLO PICASSO (1881). SKETCH FOR "LES DEMOISELLES D'AVIGNON," 1907. (30 × 20¾")
CARLO FRUA DE ANGELI COLLECTION, MILAN.

as topical sketches for the newspapers, he adjusted the subject to his inner compulsions, completely transmuting it. Thus when he reverted to earlier themes such as *The Embrace* or *Célestine*, in whose first version the woman was placed between a man and a prostitute,

PABLO PICASSO (1881). LANDSCAPE AT HORTO DE EBRO, 1909. (11 × 8¼″)
PRIVATE COLLECTION, PARIS.

all traces of realism or the anecdote were obliterated. The magnificently accurate drawing is limited to essentials; sometimes it takes the form of a simple arabesque (as in his pictures of naked children), yet it always has a sculptural plasticity. This world apart, bathed in a distinctive other-worldly light, is in the lineage of El Greco's. Nevertheless warmly human emotions find a place in it and its forms are nourished by the artist's sensibility. Thus in that poignantly expressive pastel, *The Sick Child*, a faint pink glow, like a promise of health, tinges the livid, bluish flesh. Gradually, in pursuance of this break-away from appearances, forms tend to be elongated, limbs are separated from bodies and weave an arabesque over the picture surface, and presently full, rounded curves give place to angular outlines. The *Blind Guitarist*, with his legs crossed like a Romanesque God's, the *Laundress* and the *Femme à la corneille* illustrate the extreme development of this procedure, which stems so obviously from Spanish mysticism. The last two of the pictures just mentioned were painted in the spring of 1904 after Picasso's return, for good, to Paris.

He renewed his contacts with Max Jacob and Gonzales and settled into the " Bateau-lavoir." That oddly named den of ramshackle studios in the rue Ravignan was destined to make art history. Thanks to his energy, his clear-sightedness, his mental and moral force, Picasso became the leading figure in a brilliant group including Reverdy, Raynal, Apollinaire, Braque, Derain, Gris, Gargallo and Modigliani. The story of the new art which now arose under the auspices of Cézanne forms a decisive chapter in the history of world art. Picasso had already proved his supreme gift for giving visual pleasure and stirring emotion. But he aimed higher; he knew that art implies the creation of new forms and, now he was back in Paris, explored the possibilities of a more fully integrated, architecturally ordered composition. This was his so-called " pink period " and his visit to Holland in 1905 confirmed him in his new ambition. His Schoordlam works, his big pink nudes, his *Portrait of Gertrude Stein* (1906) show a deliberate return to reality, a reality existing in its own right, independently of any emotion it arouses or any fleeting visual impression. Picasso saw it as the artist's duty to impose a stable, enduring form upon a world in perpetual flux. For this he had to discover—indeed invent—the object-in-itself, define it in time no less than in space under those permanent aspects which persist despite the metamorphoses it may undergo.

I am convinced that the rise of Cubism marked one of the two or three decisive turning-points in the history of art. Nor is there any doubt that Picasso was its originator and that however much was done by writers and poets to elucidate it and by other painters to further its discoveries, Picasso was throughout the moving spirit. Gauguin and Cézanne had only recently died when he launched the bold new venture, which despite their efforts seemed an all but hopeless quest, of giving weight and volume to the depiction of objects on a flat picture surface. To this venture he brought not only quite amazing energy, but, more important still, an open-mindedness enabling him to break with his own past, together with a practical good sense leading him to tackle each of the problems one by one, as it arose, before integrating his discoveries into an organic whole. It would seem that the physical and chemical limitations of painting do not exist for this extraordinary man. In his revealing study of Picasso's sculptures, Kahnweiler has shown how he approaches the visible world by way of the sense of touch, blocks out his representations in terms of modeling and sculpture—the basic creative art—and by actual tactile manipulation of the substances he proposes to employ. Only then does he have recourse to the means of painting in the strict sense—means of which he has a total mastery—and exploit the possibilities thus discovered. In *Les Demoiselles d'Avignon* and the series of faces painted during this period (1906) he renders the volumes with hatchings or in planes of those vivid colors to which the Fauves had recently imparted a new vibrancy, binding them with broad, rhythmical contour-lines. It is obvious that these procedures have much in common with those of certain Primitives and in particular with the marvellous creations of Negro art; indeed the newly discovered art of the Benin masks certainly encouraged Picasso in his quest of a synthetic rendering of forms.

His successive stays in Spain (at Horta de Ebro in the summer of 1909 and with Derain at Cadaquès in 1910) gave Picasso opportune reminders of the importance of employing, in his renderings of objects, landscapes and even living beings, *basic* colors, that is to say colors which owe nothing to the play of light and shade. Thus he now used a range of neutral tones in which greys, browns and earthy colors predominated, and in which even blues, pinks and greens are qualified by the juxtaposition of these neutral tints.

These are essentially the methods of analysis and it is perhaps curious that now he had got down to the basic structure of objects, Picasso felt freer to concentrate on their individual characteristics. Indeed the basic structure ended up by disappearing or rather became merely implicit, unapparent. This analytic method and a desire for absolute fidelity led him to employ elements taken from material reality itself: strips of paper, moldings, grained wood, sand and metal—thus creating what were, in effect, 'montages.' Texturally these pictures obviously approximated to sculpture. It must be admitted that this accumulation of 'real' details and also the combination on a canvas or a flat panel of different aspects of an object—a face, for instance, seen at once in profile, from behind, full-face and from above—make these pictures seem highly puzzling at first sight. Nevertheless once we have made the effort necessary to 'read' them, they are extraordinarily satisfying; never before has the essential richness of visual experience been rendered so suggestively, and somehow this unexpected congruence of all the elements implicit in what often is a quite humble theme produces an effect that is nothing short of magical. True, the visual and intellectual strain involved cannot be maintained for long either by the painter or the beholder; yet the wonderful achievements of Cubism in 1911 and 1912 compel our admiration and delight.

The upheaval caused by the first World War made a break in this creative effort. Cocteau has told us how he persuaded Picasso to come to Rome in 1917 to make the curtain and design the costumes for Satie's *Parade*, produced by Diaghileff's Russian Ballet. This was the first attempt to renovate the ballet by the association with it of the most modern art, and there is no doubt that, reciprocally, the ballet, with its symbolic gestures, influenced Picasso. During this phase he treated the acrobats and harlequins (now become musicians), the subjects of his earliest pictures, as automata, using simplified distortions suggestive of the stage and adapting them to the procedures of a Cubism of a seemingly more accessible and popularized, but none the less brilliantly effective, order.

The deep impression produced on him by Roman art probably accounts for Picasso's new manner in the years immediately after the first World War and for his pictures of luminous foreshores on which gigantic women roam. Here again we are reminded of sculpture; those big white strongly modeled figures may well owe something to the statues of antiquity. Similarly the sculptures in wrought iron and wire that he made round about 1930, along with his Spanish sculptor friend Julio Gonzalez, correspond to a period when Picasso was much interested in architectonic problems and sought to circumscribe space with lines and points without succumbing to a cold, geometrical abstractionism. Finally, in the plaster casts made at Boisgeloup in 1933 we can see the models which reappear, with hardly any changes, in the new series of paintings begun in 1934, remarkable for a vehemence of expression and richness of color that were a wholly new development in Picasso's art. Indeed the 1936 exhibition at Rosenberg's in which these huge, half savage figures were displayed caused a sensation in the Paris art world.

Since then, Picasso's art has developed simultaneously on several planes, and he often ventures, greatly daring, into realms far beyond the scope of any ordinary artist. While none better than he can reveal the underlying structure of the visible world in hieratic works governed by the austere disciplines of Cubism, he also subjects forms to the fierce distortions of his passions. He has no qualms about laying bare the most secret places of the heart; year after year he takes the same face to pieces and re-assembles it, delving even deeper than the most modern writers or psychologists. Moreover he has a gift of aloofness even from himself; the irony, diversity and elusiveness of so much of his work are indications of his open-mindedness, his accessibility to new ideas. Thus through all his chameleon-like changes he remains faithful to that instinct for self-renewal which where a great creative artist is concerned is, in the last analysis, the truest form of unity.

PABLO PICASSO (1881). THE BULL'S SKULL, 1942. (51×38″)
PRIVATE COLLECTION, PARIS.

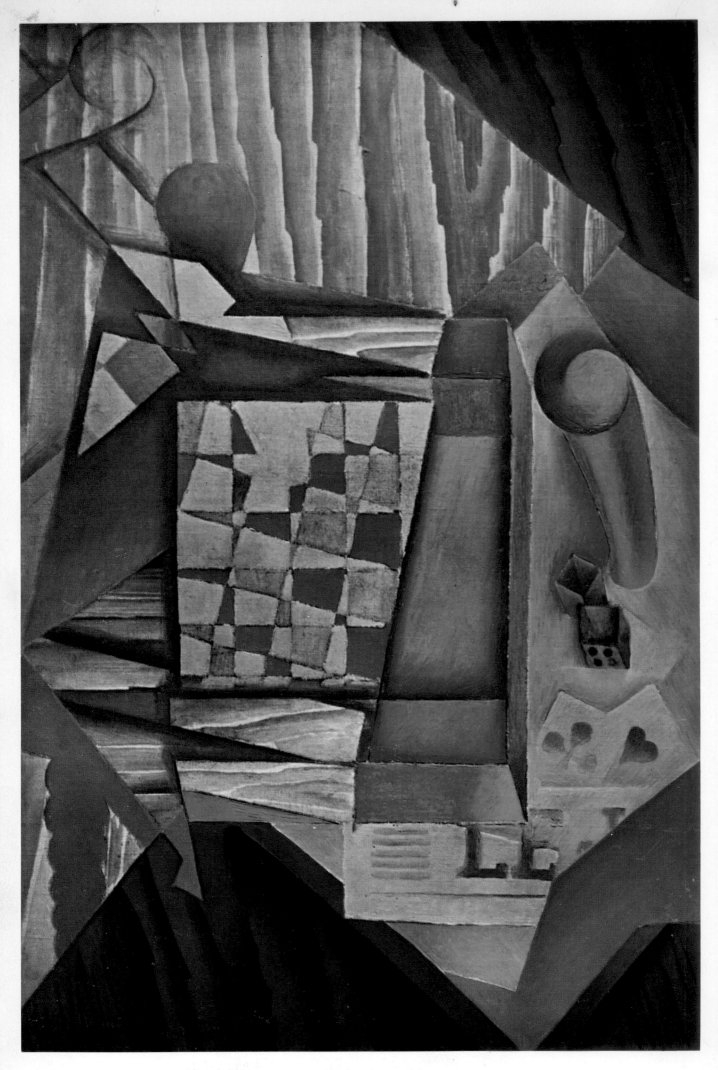

JUAN GRIS (1887-1927). BACKGAMMON, 1913. (31 ¼ × 21 ¾ ")
LOUISE LEIRIS GALLERY, PARIS.

JUAN GRIS

Though in its inception Cubism stood for a revolt against nature-imitation, the early Cubists practiced a close analysis of objects, not with a view to recording casual appearances, but so as to render all their aspects, all their facets, even cross-sections of them. That is why we find such complicated, sometimes indeed fantastic—though always expressive—juxtapositions on their canvases. These procedures obtained during the early phase of the movement, known as Analytic Cubism. Juan Gris, who came to Paris in 1906 and began by painting under the aegis of Picasso, showed from the start a desire for greater clarity and simplicity. Though his first works (exhibited in 1912) obviously belonged to Analytic Cubism, they were remarkably easy to grasp and well-balanced, this being particularly true of his portraits (the only ones he ever painted). The Cubists then had the idea of inserting in their compositions elements taken straight from reality which would help the beholder to find his way about in them; thus in his famous *Clou* Braque created illusionist effects by the use of bits of wood and marble, and very soon letters of the alphabet, strips of newspaper or wall-paper made their appearance on the picture surface.

While Juan Gris indulged in these ingenious but empirical procedures, he also thought out what was nothing short of a radical change in the whole structure of modern painting: a theory at once coherent and far-reaching. For it was he who played the leading part in the advent of what is known as Synthetic Cubism. There had already been a tendency to dissociate the compositional structure of the picture from the colors, which were sometimes tersely indicated by a mere patch or dab of pigment. This suggested that details could be treated as interchangeable without injury to the broad general effect. Starting from this premise, Gris built up a new and fruitful method, which he explained to Kahnweiler in 1920. " I begin by organizing my picture, then I ‘qualify’ the objects." Another remark he made (often quoted and usually misinterpreted) was to the effect that he proceeded from the general to the particular, from an abstraction to a real fact. The context made his meaning plain. He had begun by saying, "I work with elements of a mental order, with my imagination, and try to give concrete form to what is abstract." And added: " I want to achieve a new qualification, that is to say to construct new specific individuals, after starting off from the general type." Because elsewhere he speaks of the " mathematical architecture " of the picture, he has been regarded in some quarters as an abstract thinker who willfully reversed the normal process of artistic creation and ruled out its human element. But actually (and we have seen that Velazquez, too, proceeded in this way) the artist embarking on a new work always uses as his basis a sort of mental schema, a complex of memories and of notions that he has thought out and adapted, and consciously constructs a quasi-geometrical pattern deduced from them. Thereafter, using both his imagination and his intellect, he gives objective form to this concept so as to make it intelligible to others. Thus it is natural enough that Gris strikes us as fundamentally a classical artist; his nobly austere compositions stand for the durable and essential as against the anecdotal and ephemeral. His graphic procedures, too, are obviously carefully thought out; he employs inversions of forms (which produce something of the effect of rhymes in poetry) and also gives subtle changes of direction to his line so as to suggest volumes. Finally, his art is rich in emblems, symbols, metaphors, but without ceasing to be a logical system through and through, at once complex and coherent. Gris died when he was forty and had been painting for barely seventeen years; yet his *œuvre* has a rare perfection which well might serve as an example to the artists of today.

Amongst his followers is Maria Blanchard who was born at Santander of a Spanish father, brought up in Madrid, and came to Paris in 1908. During the war she worked with Gris at Loches, concentrating on abstract, geometric compositions. Later on, she took to realistic, sensitive depictions of the humbler, sadder aspects of life, characterized by a use of strongly defined planes played on by sudden gleams of light. Among others who learnt much from Gris may be mentioned Beaudin and the Spaniard Francisco Bores, whose elliptic art is notable for its skillfully balanced colors.

JOSÉ GUTIERREZ SOLANA (1886-1945). REUNION AT THE CAFÉ POMBO, 1920. (63 ½ × 82 ¾")
FROM LEFT TO RIGHT : MANUEL ABRIL, TOMAS BORRAS, JOSÉ BERGAMIN, CABRERO, RAMON GOMEZ DE LA SERNA,
BACARISSE, BARTOLOZZI, PEDRO LUIS COL, JOSÉ GUTIERREZ SOLANA.
MUSEUM OF MODERN ART, MADRID.

JOSÉ GUTIERREZ SOLANA

It might be interesting to determine how far those extremist, totally uninhibited manifestations of art, generally lumped together under the epithet " expressionist," stem directly from a collective subconscious rather than from the individual Ego. In this connection Solana's works are particularly revealing, for in them we find one of the constants in Spanish art—an essentially national value—making its presence felt at a time when art was steadily becoming internationalized, frontiers were ceasing to count and great art movements such as Cubism and Non-objectivism were sweeping across the Pyrenees. Nevertheless the art of José Gutierrez Solana, who was born at Madrid in 1886 and died in 1945, strikes us as wholly personal, in the sense of stemming solely from an inner compulsion and an uprush of uncontrollable forces. A lonely, isolated figure—a voice crying in the wilderness—he none the less expressed the passionate unrest and ancestral memories of a whole race, but whatever he took from the legendary lore of Spain was transmuted by his art, sublimated to an hieratic grandeur. The writers of the group known as " the men of '98 " applied themselves to diagnosing the causes of the decadence of Spain with a view to arresting it. Solana, however, far from repudiating this legacy of disaster and frustrated hopes, glimpsed in it obscure but vital significances. A gifted writer, he recorded his observations, noting all the anomalies and survivals of the past in Spanish life, and it was only after pondering deeply on these

that he took up his brush and gave them plastic expression, of an almost literal order. He immersed himself in the life of the humbler districts of Madrid and of the poverty-stricken villages of Castile, which he tirelessly explored in the diligences and ramshackle vehicles that still survived in those parts, or in squalid third-class railroad carriages. In the rustic festivals and uncouth masquerades of the peasantry he perceived rites of magic import. In Madrid he made a collection of the queerest bric-à-brac and filled his studio with fantastic curios, jetsam of the Spanish past. In the most unlikely objects he detected a secret, fascinating life and *pari passu* he imparted to living beings something of the aloofness and permanence of inanimate things: hence his predilection for large dolls, hardly distinguishable from real people. Like Goya's "black paintings," Solana's works are strangely evocative, bathed in the eerie light of some dead planet. This is essentially physical painting, imbued with a tragic, meaningful sensuality and charged with vast symbolic allusions.

Amongst the painters living in Spain who are producing experimental work of an interesting order are Daniel Vasquez Diaz, whose austere, architecturally ordered compositions (of Cubist inspiration) are remarkable for their subtle nuances of color; and Francisco Cossio, whose handling of transparent pigment evokes to perfection sealight and great gulfs of limpid air. Like the sculptor Angel Ferrant, Benjamin Palencia began (round about 1930) with tendencies towards instinctive, poetic abstraction, linked up with 'primitive' signs; subsequently he has devoted himself to the depiction of Castilian landscapes, imbuing them with spacious, lyrically emotive rhythms.

JOSÉ GUTIERREZ SOLANA (1886-1945). CHORUS GIRLS, CA. 1922. (65¼ × 83½")
MUSEUM OF MODERN ART, BARCELONA.

JOAN MIRO (1893).
THE VILLAGE OF MONTROIG, 1919. (28¾ × 24″)
OWNED BY THE ARTIST.

JOAN MIRO

More perhaps than any other modern artist Joan Miro seems an embodiment of youth and happy freedom; nevertheless his art is governed by laws of its own, a system of rhythms and harmonies that stems from his racial origin and his native soil, and which he has implemented by his extensive knowledge of primitive arts, especially the Romanesque and Pre-Romanesque arts of Catalonia. His genius has been shaped in discreet seclusion and he owes nothing to the artistic climate of his day; on the contrary he harks back across the centuries to symbols that have existed since the dawn of time and to the lost traditions of the earliest craftsmen. In his first representations of peasant life and scenes in his village we find a skillful counterpoint of colored curves, indicating the various planes with magical precision and a poetic glamour worthy of the East.

His contacts with Surrealism led Miro to dissociate these elements and re-group them differently. At first glance it may seem something of a problem, getting down to the basic themes, but as a matter of fact each can be deciphered and recognized clearly enough throughout the metamorphoses and simplifications it is made to undergo. Miro aims less at a synthesis of its various aspects than at discovering its most characteristic form, even though this may seem surprising, even grotesque. He views and reviews the model from different angles and sometimes enlarges to the maximum its most salient feature. This applies, strictly speaking, to an early phase of his development; for soon we find him using a method of " substitution," whereby the sign acquires a quasi-universal reference and no longer stems from the real world, but exists in its own right. Thus Miro has created type-

JOAN MIRO (1893). HARLEQUIN CARNIVAL, 1924-1925. (26 × 36 ½") ALBRIGHT ART GALLERY, BUFFALO, NEW YORK.

JOAN MIRO (1893). THE BIRD WITH THE CALM GAZE, ITS WINGS AFLAME, 1952. (31¾ × 39¼")
OWNED BY THE ARTIST.

forms standing for the sun, a star, a woman, a bird and so forth, and built up a new language with these hieroglyphics. Sometimes, indeed, these signs tend to become indeterminate, ambivalent, and can be interpreted only in terms of their relations to other signs. Others, again, have no concrete reference, but serve merely as accents or a sort of punctuation.

Occasionally the signs are solely spots of color standing out on a dark background, or spots of black on an illuminated background. Miro is laying an ever increasing emphasis on color, with a view to rendering his work more accessible to the beholder; for he considers that " the picture should make an immediate impact on him like a fisticuff, before reflection intervenes," and that strong colors are most effective in this respect. He builds up vast, complex, crowded compositions in which all the diverse elements that he meticulously collated in his early Catalonian landscapes are exposed and integrated on the same plane. Thus his works unfurl themselves like tapestries and give that effect of wall-decoration which he had in mind when in 1938 he asked to be given an enormous studio so that he could " transcend, so far as possible, easel painting and give the impression of vast masses of humanity." His decorations painted in the United States achieved this and were widely appreciated. In pursuit of the same aim Miro is trying to override the technical distinctions between different forms of art and in his last canvases we find elements of sculpture in relief creating a sense of depth. Thus he constructs huge mythical figures with their structure showing through, whose forms he manipulates with the utmost freedom.

SALVADOR DALI

To understand Dali the painter one must begin by trying to understand Dali the man—and both man and painter are alike exceptional and intriguing. Though he has been anything but secretive about himself in his writings (in which the self-revelations are to my mind more enlightening than the would-be philosophical notions on which the writer sets such store), Dali has been the victim of misunderstanding, and his personality cruelly misjudged. For behind the various poses he has struck and the successive masks he has thought fit to don, we can discern an underlying continuity and a very real sincerity. One of the ' constants ' of his personality has been nothing short of an obsession with the landscape of his childhood, the gaunt anatomies of the bare hills of the Ampurdan, the sandy plains and foreshores of Cadaquès dazzling white under the southern sun. That countryside of his boyhood, the most beautiful spot in the whole world as he has described it with naïve pride, is always present at the back of his mind, unforgettable and unassailable: the common denominator, so to speak, of all his divagations. Always he seems to glimpse it, through the small end of his field-glasses as he prospects the world, with its vanishing point reaching out into infinity, while in a corner of the picture the child Dali in a sailor-suit, hoop in hand, sets the scale of some monstrous composition.

This persistence of infantile traits at once explains and to some extent humanizes Dali's often irritating mannerisms. For him, painting is both memory in action and a vehicle for the poet's vision. He was an intimate friend of Federico Garcia Lorca in his youth and this association involved a constant testing out of their respective inspirations, each seeking to outdo the other, in friendly rivalry. Lorca, too, tried his hand at sketching and produced paintings of a gossamer-light fantasy. Against these Dali set up concrete plastic forms, carrying his devotion to meticulous exactitude to the point of illusionist realism. He even had recourse to photography, whose possibilities he was subsequently to explore to such sensational effect in the films on which he collaborated, *Le Chien Andalou* and *L'Age d'or*.

Though Dali's attitude to life and art was wholly anarchic, he personally was methodical and painstaking and as an art-student at Madrid he conscientiously assimilated the academic teachings of Moreno Carbonero. He was a voracious reader of Freud and philosophical treatises, while at the same time following eagerly, by way of the art magazines, the latest developments of Cubism, Futurism and Metaphysical Painting. The works he exhibited in Barcelona at Dalmau's and also in Madrid—at the first Exhibition of Iberian Artists, in which Ferrant, Palencia, Cossio and Bores also figured—were already marked by a characteristic nostalgia and a predilection for strong contrasts. After a brief dalliance with Cubism, Dali won through to his own world, a world of vast recessions, luminous sea spaces glimpsed through shadowed windows, with women in the foreground leaning their elbows on the sills.

Yet, given his restless temperament, this balanced vision could not wholly satisfy him. He went to Paris, met Picasso, joined forces with the Surrealists, persuaded his new friends to come to Cadaquès, organized a successful exhibition at the Galerie Goemans, and married Gala Eluard. This was the time when the Surrealists were making their first " purge " and breaking with Masson, Soupault, Leiris and Desnos. After the way of neophytes Dali was full of zeal and pugnacity; with a great spate of philosophical terminology he launched a new method of creation that he styled " paranoiac-critical." The idea was to institute a permanent state of psychological disturbance by stepping up the artist's sensibility to fever pitch, and to promote a deliberate, systematic exploitation of " objects functioning symbolically." And, in fact, he showed great personal skill in employing hallucinations, the vagaries of memory and all the distortions of visual experience suggested by a close study of psychological aberrations and pathological disorders. By fixing one's eye on any given object one may induce a sort of hypnosis and this to Dali's thinking was a pointer for the artist; by concentrating on some object in the outside world he is enabled simultaneously to express the obsession it exercises on him and to liberate his subconscious from this obsession and the object itself from its normal connotation.

Dali sought both to transcend and to exhaust the utmost possibilities of the real in a single operation. The basic elements in his pictures are objects reproduced in the most mechanical manner, such as snapshots of figures or faces "taken" in their most fleeting, least expressive moments, or *clichés* of wholly conventional paintings like Millet's *Angelus*. The next step was to make this image undergo a sort of decomposition, manifested by the softening up or elongation of its structure, or indicated in a yet more obvious way by swarms of flies or visible signs of putrefaction. The effect of this procedure was to displace the normal significance of the object, making of it something new and strange.

When in 1937-1938 Dali came under the influence of the Italian Renaissance and the return to Classicism evident in his recent works set in, he was venturing on more dangerous ground and his future seemed precarious. His former friends repudiated him and Breton denounced his technique as "ultra-retrograde." Indeed despite the vast success which, like another Fortuny, he had in the United States, Dali might well have found this venture was leading him up a blind alley, had not his return to Spain enabled him to find congenial nourishment for that basic realism combined with graphic fantasy which links him up with the great tradition of Spanish Baroque art.

SALVADOR DALI (1904). THE SPECTER OF SEX APPEAL, 1937. (7 × 5 ½″)
OWNED BY THE ARTIST.

BIOGRAPHICAL
AND
BIBLIOGRAPHICAL NOTICES
BY
A. BUSUIOCEANU

INDEX OF NAMES

BIOGRAPHIES

ANTOLIÑEZ, JOSÉ (1635-1675).

This painter, whose career was a brief one, was the most brilliant pupil to come out of Francisco Rizi's school. Born at Madrid in 1635, a carpenter's son, he persistently laid claim to the title of 'hidalgo,' which in the end he secured. He is thought to have begun his art studies under a little known Madrid painter, J. G. Benavides, whose daughter he married in 1653, before he was 18. His lot was not easy ; he never succeeded in making ends meet, but was inordinately proud, keen-witted, sharp-tongued. A sparkling colorist, especially fond of bright tones and harmonies of silvery blues and greys, he no doubt profited from a study of Veronese and was also attracted by Van Dyck. His earliest dated works (1663) are a *St John the Baptist* (Cathedral of Valencia) and an *Immaculate Conception* (Prado). Highly successful with the latter theme, he treated it in several versions. However, his *Martyrdom of St Sebastian* (Cerralbo Museum, Madrid), painted in 1667, is technically superior to these. Dating from the same year is a picture, now in the Copenhagen Museum, containing portraits of several Danish personalities. In the Munich Pinakothek is a fine *Immaculate Conception* by Antoliñez, dated 1668, and another, even better one, is in the Lazaro Museum, Madrid, dated 1675. There are also swooning *Magdalens* by him in the Prado and in the former Royal Gallery of Rumania. An excellent genre picture in the Alte Pinakothek, Munich, known as *The Poor Painter*, and containing the artist's self-portrait, shows us a man of shrewd and ready wit, while there are touches both of humor and melancholy in the general presentation. A quite exceptional man in every way, Antoliñez died at the early age of 40 in 1675.

CANO, ALONSO (1601-1667).

Few artists' lives have been stormier than Alonso Cano's. A vain, proud, irascible man constantly at odds with those around him, he seems to have painted by way of relaxation between the dramatic crises and quarrels that marked his career. Born at Granada in 1601, he no doubt got his first lessons from his father, a designer and builder of retables. In 1614 father and son moved to Seville and in 1616 Cano was Velazquez' fellow-student under Pacheco. 1626 saw him a qualified master doing sculpture and painting at Seville, where he had already made his name. Dating from this time is his *St Inez* (Berlin) ; its style is one of almost rude simplicity reminiscent of Zurbaran, who in fact had just settled at Seville and whose success aroused Cano's hostility. In 1638, while working chiefly as a sculptor, he was forced to make a sudden move to Madrid as the result of a duel with another artist. There, thanks to Velazquez, he was patronized by the Count-Duke Olivares and taken into the King's service as—among other functions—drawing-master to the Infante Baltasar Carlos. Set to work restoring pictures by Titian and Rubens damaged in a fire at the Palace in 1640, he now studied the great Italian and Flemish masters in the royal collections, notably Van Dyck. He was commissioned in 1643 to do a series of portraits of former kings for the Palace of Madrid ; three of these, now in the Prado, have an agreeable geniality and show signs of Flemish influence. But this tranquil period of his life was of short duration : in 1644 his wife died under mysterious circumstances and Cano was arrested by the Inquisition. Hardly had his trial

N. B. - The biographies of El Greco, Pacheco and Ribalta are to be found in the first volume of our *SPANISH PAINTING*, FROM THE CATALAN FRESCOS TO EL GRECO.

begun than he thought it wiser to make an escape. (The records of this trial, which were available until quite recently in the Spanish National Archives but never published, have unfortunately disappeared.) He now roamed about for some time, always on the move. In 1645 he did some paintings for the church of Getafe, a village near Madrid. Finally, in 1649, he was able to resume his Court functions. In 1651 his appointment as *racionero* (intendant) of the Granada Cathedral gave rise to protests ; feeling ran high against him and bickerings continued for the next ten years. But Cano won out in the end, thanks to royal patronage, and settled for good at Granada in 1660. Between 1652 and 1664 he painted a cycle of pictures at the Granada Cathedral, *The Seven Joys of Mary* ; though they are of unequal value and show little real inspiration, these are his chief works. On the strength of them Cano has been assigned, suitably enough, a place midway between Guido Reni and Murillo.

CARREÑO DE MIRANDA, JUAN (1614-1685).

We can hardly speak of a successor to Velazquez, though officially his post at the Spanish Court, under Charles II, fell to Juan Carreño de Miranda, an Asturian painter born at Avilés in 1614. Early biographers name the painters Pedro de las Cuevas and Bartolomé Roman as his masters in Madrid. More recent authors surmise he may have studied first at Valladolid. However this may be, Carreño's real masters were Velazquez and Van Dyck, whom he zealously copied. A friend of Francisco Rizi, with whom he often collaborated, he was presented at Court by Velazquez during the reign of Philip IV. In 1655 he was employed on painting frescos in the Hall of Mirrors of the Royal Palace. But it was not until somewhat later, under Charles II, that he was given official status, becoming 'Pintor de Camara' in 1669 and King's Painter in 1671. From this time on, he was the favorite artist of the royal family, particularly esteemed by Charles II and the Queen Mother, Doña Mariana. His career is generally divided into two periods. Beginning as a religious painter and decorator, he painted Immaculate Conceptions and Assumptions which met with great success ; they are very different from those of Murillo, both in the Baroque movement of the forms and their vigorous color. During his second period Carreño devoted himself chiefly to the portrait. Impressed by his refined use of color and the elegance he imparts to his models, critics have seen in him a Spanish Van Dyck ; however, the fluency of his execution, a noticeable freedom in his brushwork and the composition of his palette indicate, rather, his debt to Velazquez. In his many portraits of Charles II and Doña Mariana, he displayed great psychological shrewdness in rendering the frail, sickly figure of the 'bewitched King' and the pallid melancholy of the Queen, dressed as a nun in all these portraits.

COELLO, CLAUDIO (1642-1693).

Coello is the last great name of the Madrid XVIIth-century school. Of Portuguese extraction, he was born at Madrid in 1642. His father, a bronze-worker, hoped to see his son follow the same *métier* and apprenticed him to Francisco Rizi's studio to learn the rudiments of drawing. It was not long before Rizi noticed the boy's exceptional gifts and taught him the secrets of his essentially Baroque art, full of fire, but weak in technique. Coello was still Rizi's pupil when, in 1663, he gained his first success with some showy paintings which he made for the Convent of San Placido at Madrid. Two other pictures from the same period—the *Holy Family* (1660) and the *Triumph of St Augustine*

(1664), both at the Prado—display the same exuberant imagination, vivacious color and excellent draftsmanship. Though his technique was already more advanced than his master's, he did not give up his studies. Thanks to his friendship with Carreño he had access to the Royal Collections and he made many copies, notably of the works of Titian, Rubens and Van Dyck. He also learnt the technique of fresco painting from José Donoso and the two painters worked together in the Cathedral of Toledo (1671) and in many churches and buildings in and around Madrid. Coello later worked by himself in the Augustinian Convent of La Manteria at Saragossa (1683). He specialized in huge, intricate compositions that enabled him to come to grips with a variety of technical problems and display his virtuosity. Coello was highly thought of by Charles II, who in 1683 bestowed on him the honorary title of King's Painter. He was appointed ' Pintor de Camara ' upon the death of Carreño in 1685, and employed on decorative works in the Palace and painting portraits of the royal family. His outstanding work, however, is the large painting he did for the sacristy of the Escorial in 1685-1686, representing the *Adoration of the Sacred Form*. The artist was now in high favor with the King and universally esteemed. But he was over-ready to take offence and could not endure any competition on the part of other artists. Thus, in 1689, upon the death of the Queen, Marie-Louise de Bourbon, it was a cruel blow for him when the architect José Churriguera was chosen to execute the funeral decorations. His world collapsed in 1692 when the Neapolitan painter Luca Giordano, the famous *Fa presto*, arrived in Madrid and was invited to work in the Escorial. Contemporary witnesses assure us that it was due to chagrin at these fancied or real slights that Coello died in 1693.

COTAN, Fray Juan SANCHEZ (1561-1624).

Beside men of El Greco's or Ribalta's stature, this modest but genuinely gifted painter cuts the figure of a XVIIth-century Flemish ' little master,' conscientiously devoting himself to still lifes and pious subjects. He was born at Orgaz, in La Mancha, in 1561, and studied at Toledo under a little known painter, Blas del Prado. From the start he showed familiarity with the new methods of ' Tenebrism,' which he employed to great effect in his ' bodegones ' (one of them dated 1602), the most significant of which is that known as *The Teasel*, often imitated and now to be seen in the Museum of Granada. He became a monk in 1604, entering the Carthusian monastery at Paular, in Castile ; thence in 1612 he migrated to the Carthusian monastery at Granada. His best religious pictures are the murals in the cloister of this monastery (1615-1617), illustrating the lives of St Bruno and other saints. In another work, his *Vision of St Francis*, at the Cathedral of Seville (1620), we find traces of Roelas' influence. He died in his monastery at Granada in 1624.

DALI, Salvador (1904).

Born at Figueras, near Barcelona, he enrolled at the Madrid School of Fine Arts in 1921, but his unruly conduct led to his expulsion in 1924. Drawn at first to Chirico's and Carrà's " metaphysical " style and then to Cubism, he took part in the Exhibition of Iberian Artists at Madrid in 1925 and had a one-man show at Barcelona, where his meticulous technique based on expert draftsmanship attracted much attention. On his first visit to Paris in 1928 he met Picasso and the Surrealists, and became an adept of Surrealism. He exhibited at the Goemans Gallery, Paris, in 1929, wrote poems in Spanish and published (in French) *La femme visible* and also *L'Amour et la mémoire* in 1930. In 1931 he collaborated with Buñuel on the film *L'Age d'or*. His interpretations of *William*

Tell and Millet's *Angélus* date from 1931-1934. He illustrated Lautréamont's *Chants de Maldoror* (1934). With a trip to Italy in 1937 began his conversion to the art principles of the Renaissance. In 1940 he settled in the United States and next year had a retrospective exhibition at the Museum of Modern Art, New York. He published his autobiography *The Secret Life of Salvador Dali* in 1944. *The Madonna of Port Lligat*, a large panel painted in 1950, illustrates his new manner, inspired by Raphael and Luca Paccioli. Dali has set forth his views in a *Mystical Manifesto*, published in 1951. Revisiting Spain in 1951, he gave a lecture at Madrid entitled *Picasso and I*.

ESQUIVEL, Antonio Maria (1806-1857).

This painter is a good representative of the romantic period in Spain, under Isabella II. Born at Seville in 1806, he spent his youth in poverty amid the hardships of war and himself joined the army at 17, taking part in the siege of Cadiz and the defense of the Trocadero. He had begun studying art at an early age in Seville, where he was taught to imitate Murillo. In 1831 he moved to Madrid and continued his studies at the Academy of San Fernando. To earn a living he painted scenes of Andalusian life and made copies of Murillo which he sold to picture-dealers. But now he also began to do portraits. In 1837 he was one of the founders of the *Liceo artistico y literario*, the headquarters of the romantic movement in Madrid. His reputation was now established and he was the intimate friend of many well-known writers. Suddenly, however, as a result of an illness, Esquivel lost his eyesight. At Seville he made two attempts at suicide, but his friends stood by him loyally, giving him both material aid and moral encouragement. Then, almost miraculously, he recovered his sight. For a time he devoted himself to religious painting. He later returned to portrait-painting, the genre in which we see him at his best. His portraits are scrupulously lifelike, but his execution was sensitive and he had a delicate feeling for color. His approach was simple and direct and his pictures of his friends, bourgeois, artists, and writers, are full of kindly understanding. He died in Madrid in 1857.

FORTUNY, Mariano (1838-1874).

Born at Reus (Catalonia) in 1838, he began studying art at Barcelona in 1852 and joined the Catalonian ' Nazarenes,' Lorenzale and Mila. He was also attracted by Gavarni's prints. In 1858 he went to Rome on a scholarship, and next year was sent to Morocco to record incidents of the war. There he took to painting those North African scenes which were among the factors of his success. He went to Paris in 1860, then back to Morocco in 1862. Goupil discovered him and launched him on the international picture market. The famous picture-dealer encouraged him to paint scenes of the kind then in great demand, small pictures, brilliantly and meticulously executed, on themes of the *ancien régime*. Fortuny soon established himself as a master and now proceeded to launch his Spanish subjects. He was so highly thought of that Meissonier himself consented to sit for his picture, *La Vicaria* (Barcelona), which was sold by Goupil in 1870 at a fabulous price. That year Fortuny returned to Spain, made another trip to Morocco, then settled in Italy ; he died in Rome in 1874, aged only 36.

GOYA Y LUCIENTES, Francisco (1746-1828).

In 1800 the Academy of San Fernando in Madrid published Cean Bermudez' six-volume *Historical Dictionary of the Most Illustrious Professors of Fine Arts in Spain*. The work contained no mention of Goya, then in his 55th year, a member of the Academy of San Fernando and favorite painter at the Court. Perhaps he was overlooked precisely because he loomed so large! But of course dictionaries of this kind are notorious for stupendous oversights. Goya was born in 1746 at Fuendetodos, near Saragossa, in Aragon, a province that had never produced a great painter. A gilder's son, at 14 he was apprenticed to the studio of José Luzan, a Saragossa painter. The boy was far from precocious but he had his mind set on studying at the Madrid Academy. Presenting himself in 1763, he was rejected. A second attempt in 1766 met with the same result. Undaunted, he resolved to train himself, while keeping an eye on the masters of the day: the Italian Tiepolo, then working in Madrid, the German Mengs, and his fellow Aragonese Francisco Bayeu. He made a trip to Italy on his own in 1769 or 1770, and worked in Rome, then at Parma where he entered a competition and won second prize with a picture of the theme of *Hannibal crossing the Alps*. Thus when he went back to Saragossa he had a certain standing and obtained a few commissions, though minor ones. As ambitious as ever, he returned to Madrid in 1775, this time with better luck. He married Bayeu's sister, and thus made useful contacts; through these, and thanks to Mengs' good offices, he was commissioned in 1776 to do some cartoons for the Royal Tapestry Factory. He worked hard at this until 1790, making his name with decorative compositions depicting popular scenes of Madrid life, launching the new genre and style known today as " Goyesque." In 1780 he was appointed King's Painter and entered the Academy the same year. His relations with Bayeu got him the commission for some frescos at the Saragossa Cathedral (1780-1781); but Goya never finished these, as Bayeu's high-handed attitude led to an estrangement between the two men. On his return to Madrid Goya did some religious pictures for San Francisco el Grande. But it was his genius as a portraitist that brought him into prominence and he became much sought after by the highest circles in Madrid. He became friendly with the Duke and Duchess of Osuna, then with the Duchess of Alba, immortalized in his portraits. This was the happiest period of his life. He became assistant director of painting at the Academy in 1785, Court Painter in 1786, ' Pintor de Camara ' to Charles IV in 1789; the summer of 1790 saw his triumphal trip to Valencia. But years of trial were at hand. Attacked by a nervous disease, he recovered in 1794, but was left stone deaf. This was the end of his happy years but the beginning of his great creative achievement, and the awakening of his turbulent genius, nourished by solitude, meditation and his far-ranging imagination. He continued painting portraits and now reached the peak of his so-called " silver period." At the same time he began that brilliant series of portraits of Charles IV and Queen Maria Luisa in which his mastery so often verges on the cruelest satire: *The Family of Charles IV* (Prado 1800) is their epitome. The previous year Goya had been raised to the rank of first ' Pintor de Camara.' During this time (1798-1799) he also did the frescos in the chapel of San Antonio de la Florida (Madrid), a delightful, almost literal transcription of everyday life in Madrid, a theme that had never failed to inspire him. The same year (1799) he published the complete edition of his *Caprichos*—only to withdraw it two days after it went on sale when the Inquisition, again in power, showed signs of displeasure. The Napoleonic invasion, the popular uprising and the collapse of the monarchy failed to interrupt Goya's creative activity. He retained his post at the Palace under successive régimes, but what he really thought of things is recorded in his work, which eloquently expresses his repulsion for all forms of inhumanity and tyranny. His etchings of *The Disasters of War*, done in 1808, 1812 and 1819, the numerous drawings which preceded them, and such pictures (in the Prado) as *The Charge of the Mamelukes at the*

Puerta del Sol and *The Shootings of May Third*— all bear witness to his deep emotional participation in the events of the day. Another series of etchings, the *Bull Fights* of 1815, momentarily shows again his fondness for popular sights and scenes. But solitude claimed him more and more; living in seclusion in his country house near Madrid, he gave himself up to expressing the specters of his memory and imagination, concealing nothing of their savagery. The series of *Disparates*, supreme manifestation of his genius as an etcher, dates from 1819. Another culmination came with the ' black paintings,' with which he decorated his house (these are now in the Prado). The state of his health and the troubled political conditions then prevailing at Madrid led him to spend his last years in voluntary exile. He moved to France in 1824 and after a brief stay in Paris settled at Bordeaux. In the tranquil atmosphere of his home there, he developed a new handling of color, using a brighter, more subtly composed palette than ever before—and thus becoming the true pioneer of modern painting. He died at Bordeaux in 1828, aged 82.

GRIS, JUAN (1887-1927).

Thirteenth son of a well-to-do Madrid tradesman, Gris (whose real name was José Victoriano Gonzalez) was born in that city in 1887. At 15 he entered the Madrid School of Arts and Crafts and was first influenced by the ' Jugendstil,' examples of which he saw (ca. 1904) in the German magazines *Jugend* and *Simplicissimus*. He did illustrations for a magazine, *Madrid Comico*, then in 1906 went to Paris, met Picasso and settled in the *Bateau-lavoir*. He soon met Apollinaire, Max Jacob and André Salmon, contributed drawings to *L'Assiette au Beurre*, *Le Charivari*, *Le Cri de Paris*, *Témoin* and adopted the pseudonym Juan Gris. After 1910 he devoted himself heart and soul to painting, exhibiting for the first time in 1912 at the Salon des Indépendants and then at the Section d'Or. His first *papiers collés* and *Homage to Picasso* date from 1912. The summer of 1913 saw him at Céret with Picasso, 1914 at Collioure with Matisse and Marquet. He illustrated Reverdy's *Poèmes en prose* (1915). His friendship with Picasso had involved him in Cubism from the outset, but alongside Picasso and Braque he evolved his own style, one of ever-increasing purism and severity, based on intellectual speculation. During his period of ' architectural color,' which began in 1916, he developed his colorism and sought to reduce the human figure to purely pictorial terms in his *Harlequins* and *Pierrots*, a series begun in 1919. In 1920 he took part in the last group exhibition of the Cubists and began his ' poetic painting,' an attempt to employ color in terms of the laws of rhythm; his ' polyphonic ' period followed in 1924. In the same year he gave a lecture at the Sorbonne: *On the Possibilities of Painting*, a closely reasoned statement of Cubist theory. He died of uremia in 1927 at Boulogne-sur-Seine.

HERRERA EL VIEJO, FRANCISCO (1576?-1656).

The part played by Herrera the Elder in shaping the XVIIth-century School of Seville has probably been over-emphasized. It is true that his art marks a break with the worn-out Mannerism of such painters as Pacheco, but he did not influence his contemporaries to any very great extent, nor can a single picture by him properly be called a masterpiece. Tradition has it he was born at Seville in 1576, but there are grounds for thinking he was born ten years later. His first dated work is an engraving done in 1609. He had a special gift for this technique —and in fact turned it to account by producing counterfeit money, with the result that he was soon in trouble with the authorities. He saved the situation by hurriedly entering the Jesuit

Order of San Hermenegildo at Seville, where he worked for some time. Legend has it that his *Apotheosis* of this saint (now in the Museum of Seville) so much impressed King Philip IV when he visited the Jesuit college in 1624 that he pardoned the artist. In any event, the work itself is a notable one in Herrera's output, for together with the *Vision of St Basil* (Museum of Seville) and *St Basil* (Louvre), it illustrates the first phase of the artist's mature style. A few years later he was at work with Zurbaran on a cycle of paintings for the Church of St Bonaventure at Seville, illustrating the life of the saint (1629). The three pictures which Herrera contributed to this cycle (one of them is in the Prado) are handled with much energy. The artist settled at Madrid in 1650 and died there in 1656. Herrera was Velazquez' first teacher, though only for a short time, it seems, as the pupil was unable to endure for long the asperities of his hot-tempered master, and much preferred the kindlier instruction of Pacheco, Herrera is a typical example of what the Spanish call *mal genio*. His son Francisco, also a painter and known as Herrera el Mozo (the Younger), ran away from home and fled to Italy, though not before robbing his father of all he could lay his hands on. Herrera's daughter, naturally enough perhaps, withdrew from the world and entered a convent.

LOPEZ Y PORTANA, VICENTE (1772-1850).

Spanish painting took a backward step with Lopez, Goya's official successor and universal favorite with the fashionable world of Madrid in the time of Ferdinand VII and Isabella II. Born at Valencia in 1772 and a disciple of Maella at Madrid, he faithfully followed the academic methods prescribed by Mengs a quarter of a century before. In 1814 Ferdinand VII appointed him First Painter of the Court, Director General of the Academy in 1817 and then Conservator of the Prado. Himself a model of industry, he was seconded by his sons and pupils. He painted the allegorical frescos at the Palace of the Orient, Madrid, religious pictures and a prodigious number of portraits, a pageant of the faces and showy attire of the leading figures of the day. This brilliant Madrid society, so full of life and interest in Goya's pictures, seems suddenly to age and lose its personality in those of his official successor. Too much absorbed in rendering details and appearance, Lopez never got down to the essentials.

LUCAS PADILLA, EUGENIO (1824-1870).

Goya did not inaugurate a school in Spain ; he had merely some belated imitators, most skillful of whom was Eugenio Lucas, born in 1824 at Alcala de Henares. Almost a self-taught artist, he took only a few desultory lessons at the Academy and trained himself by copying Velazquez and Goya at the Prado. He had no contacts with officialdom, made no effort to keep in the public eye and devoted himself to genre painting. Though he made some romantic landscapes in the manner of his brother-in-law, Perez Villamil, his subjects were usually those favored by Goya—Inquisition scenes, bull-fights, majas, public fêtes, episodes of warfare and the like ; in these he showed much facility and brio. He stayed in Paris in 1852, in Italy and Switzerland, and in 1859 in Morocco, where he painted in the manner of Fortuny. His death in Madrid in 1870 passed unnoticed by the art critics and authorities. He was 'discovered' much later when it was realized that his paintings figured in many collections and museums abroad, often under Goya's name. Today there are even some fake Lucases !

MAYNO, FRAY JUAN BAUTISTA (1585-86?-1649).

Of Italian origin, Mayno was born near Milan about 1585-1586. Records first mention him as being at Toledo in 1611. There he joined the Dominican Order, and entered the monastery of St Peter Martyr. Some years later, he became drawing master to the Infante, the future King Philip IV, for whom he sometimes acted as an adviser on art matters. It was he, in 1627, who judged the competition in which Velazquez, Carducho and Nardi took part. His major work is a group of pictures done in 1612 for the High Altar of St Peter Martyr ; these are now divided between the Prado *(The Adoration of the Magi)* and the Museums of Villanueva y Geltru and Toledo. The colors, if rather cold, are brilliant, sometimes glittering, and with effects of chiaroscuro. In the same style, with typically Spanish realism, are the Jeronimos *Pentecost* at Madrid and the *Adoration of the Shepherds* at the Hermitage, Leningrad. Mayno's bright manner can be seen in his huge picture of *The Reconquest of the Bay of San Salvador* (Prado), a work difficult to date, but probably subsequent to 1635. Mayno's œuvre includes a number of portraits. He died at Madrid in 1649.

MIRO, JOAN (1893).

Born at Montroig, near Tarragona, he entered the School of Fine Arts in 1907 and in 1912 the Gali Academy at Barcelona. After 1915 he worked on his own. He exhibited for the first time at Dalmau's in Barcelona in 1918. Visiting Paris in 1919, he met Picasso and was influenced by Cubism, practicing at the same time a graphic style with a tendency towards a poetic rendering of visual experience. Cubist influence persisted in his *Still Lifes* of 1920, compositions in flat planes that stressed linear arabesques and were notable for their vivid colors. In 1921, presented by Maurice Raynal, he exhibited at the La Licorne Gallery, Paris. Dating from 1922 is *The Farm* (Ernest Hemingway Collection), a picture that sums up this period of symbolic imagery and poetic treatment of nature. Miro embraced Surrealism and exhibited at the Pierre Gallery in 1925. He worked for the Russian ballet, with Max Ernst, and took part in the first group exhibition of the Surrealists at the Pierre Gallery. After a trip to Holland (1928) and an exhibition at Brussels (1929), he showed for the first time in New York (1930). A poll of American children on the painter and picture they liked best brought an almost unanimous answer : Miro and his *Dutch Interior* (1928). Breton wrote that " he is probably the most surrealistic of us all " *(Le surréalisme et la peinture)*. In 1934 he began a ' pure ' period of total simplification and abstraction (though his titles remained quite concrete). After the occupation of France in 1940, Miro returned to Barcelona, where he worked with the ceramist Artigas and did lithographs. During a trip to America in 1947 he painted a mural decoration at Cincinnati ; the early phases in which the work was built up were filmed in colors by Thomas Bouchars. Today the artist is in active production, dividing his time between Barcelona and Paris.

MURILLO, BARTOLOMÉ ESTEBAN (1618-1682).

There is no satisfactory biography of this painter, once regarded as the Raphael of Spanish art. His glory has undergone so complete an eclipse in our time, however, that modern critics, even in Spain, are seldom minded to study his life and work. Murillo was born at Seville in 1618, when Zurbaran and Velazquez were starting their careers. An orphan at the age of ten, he was looked after by an uncle who had him enrolled in the studio of Juan del Castillo. We know little of the influences which went to shape his art. It has never been proved that he traveled, to Madrid or elsewhere and it may be that he never left his native Andalusia. In this case the obvious Flemish and Venetian elements in his art may be explained by the presence in Seville of collections containing works of these schools. Murillo's first notable success was with the series of pictures he painted in 1645-

1646 for the Franciscan Convent of Seville. Among them, that representing *The Charity of San Diego of Alcala* (now at the San Fernando Academy, Madrid) is a good example of what has been called his *frio* or "cold" style. Already, however, a picture in the same series, the famous *Angels' Kitchen* (Louvre, signed 1646) foreshadowed a warmer manner and richer effects of chiaroscuro. By the middle of the century Murillo had solidly established himself and was kept busy filling the orders that poured into his studio. His style continually gained in suppleness, combining almost feminine, Andalusian grace with candid realism, steeped, however, in an atmosphere of suavity and sentiment. Pictures like the *Holy Family with a Bird* (Prado) and the *Last Supper* (Santa Maria la Blanca, Seville, dated 1650) still betray the influence of Ribera and the *tenebrosi* in general, whereas his *Sts Isidoro and Leandro* (Cathedral of Seville) and *Birth of the Virgin* (Louvre), one of his finest works, have a fluent style and delicacy of color that contrast sharply with the art of such of his contemporaries as Zurbaran. In the enormous *Vision of St Anthony* (Cathedral of Seville, 1656), Murillo handled the problems of chiaroscuro with an insight and mastery that bring Rembrandt to mind. From this time on his palette had all the attributes of his best style. Using these to the full and deftly filtering his color through alternations of light and shadow, he created in 1665 two authentic masterpieces : the pictures, now at the Prado, illustrating the legend of the *Founding of Santa Maria Maggiore in Rome*. Also among his leading works are the picture sequences he did at Seville for the Capuchin Convent (1665-1670) and the church of the Hospital of the Caridad (1670-1674). Apart from these a huge number of Murillo's works are housed in museums and private collections. The artist owed much of his popularity to his *Madonnas* and *Immaculate Conceptions*. His genre pieces are also famous ; good examples of these can be seen at the Louvre, the Munich Pinakothek, the Hermitage, Leningrad, and the National Gallery, London. Murillo was also an excellent portraitist. His last work, a large-scale rendering of the *Betrothal of St Catherine*, is in the Capuchin Convent at Cadiz. The artist had nearly finished this picture when he fell from the scaffolding upon which he was working ; the accident proved fatal, and he died in 1682.

NONELL, ISIDRO (1872-1911).

This artist was a precursor of the new movement in painting that began in Catalonia in the early 1900's. Born at Barcelona, he started off with sketches of a realistic order that heralded a reaction against the 'genteel modernism' of such men as Santiago Rusiñol and Ramon Casas. He had his first one-man show in 1896. Next year he exhibited drawings in Paris at the Desbourg Gallery, in 1899 at Vollard's, and attracted some attention. Steinlen, Daumier and Lautrec influenced him at this time. Returning to Barcelona—where Picasso now was coming on the scene—he became the undisputed leader of the group of artists who forgathered at the "4 Gats." Devoting himself to figure painting, he sought his models among gipsies and the down-and-out characters of Barcelona low life, using these themes to deepen his study of colors, which in his pictures are always somber and heavy, though vaguely bathed in a golden sheen. He now became interested in the rendering of volume and in his last years painted some fine still lifes. Nonell's Barcelona exhibition in 1910 was a triumph ; but he died in the following year.

PARET Y ALCAZAR, LUIS (1746-1799).

Goya's contemporary, this excellent painter, who was especially drawn to minor genres, plainly shows the influence of French art. Born at Madrid

in 1746, he began his art studies at a very early age, first under Antonio Gonzalez Velazquez, then under the French painter who was to be his true master, Charles-François de la Traverse, a disciple of Boucher. He painted the *fêtes* and ceremonies of the Bourbon Court in Madrid. He was commissioned by the King to make a series of pictures for the Palace of the Orient illustrating the ports of Spain. He also made illustrations for the works of Cervantes and Quevedo. He died in Madrid in 1799.

PICASSO, PABLO RUIZ (1881).

Picasso was born at Malaga. His father, who came from the Basque country, was an art-teacher ; his mother was Andalusian. In 1891 the family moved to Corunna, where Picasso (at the age of ten) made his first drawings. He started painting four years later at Barcelona ; 1897 saw his first exhibition and the first article on his work (in *La Vanguardia*). The same year, as a pupil of Muñoz Degrain, he took part in the National Exhibition in Madrid with a picture called *Science and Charity*. But he took no more interest in the Academy at Madrid than he had at Barcelona, and studied on his own in the Prado. Returning to Barcelona, he found a congenial group in the writers and artists who congregated at the 'Els Quatre Gats' café. Late in 1900 he made his first visit to Paris, then came back to Madrid where, in 1901, he launched a short-lived review, *Arte Joven*. From now on he signed his pictures 'Picasso' instead of 'Ruiz Picasso.' During visits to Paris in 1901 and 1902 he exhibited at Vollard's (1901) and at Berthe Weill's (1902), and met Max Jacob. He began his 'blue' period in 1901, which he continued in Barcelona in 1902-1903, and painted his first harlequins (1903). He settled for good in Paris in 1904 at the *Bateau-lavoir*, rue Ravignan, where he had his studio for the next five years. During this difficult phase he met Apollinaire, haunted circuses and did the 16 etchings called *The Tumblers* (1904-1905), published in 1913 by Vollard. His 'pink' period began in 1905, with a return to more classical forms after a trip to Holland. He met Matisse in 1906 and painted his *Portrait of Gertrude Stein* in which he seems to seek more realistic effects, under a synthetic form. With *Les Demoiselles d'Avignon* (1906-1907) he broke entirely new ground, inspired by Ivory Coast masks. Apollinaire introduced him to Braque (1907) and the dealer Kahnweiler made a contract for all his work. In 1908 at the *Bateau-lavoir* Picasso gave the famous banquet in honor of the Douanier Rousseau. A decisive phase began with stays at Horta de Ebro (1909), at Cadaquès with Derain (1901), at Céret with Braque (1911) and at Sorgues (1912), and with Cubism painting was given a new direction. In his 1914-1915 pictures Picasso used bright, flat colors. Soon after, when Jean Cocteau persuaded him to go to Rome and do the sets and costumes for Diaghilev's *Parade*, the ballet provided him with a new source of inspiration. This stay in Rome had other consequences : in 1920, without abandoning his other styles, Picasso started his neo-classical period, painting gigantic women seated beside the sea. Inspired by sculpture, he gave his painting a monumental turn. Later, under the influence of Surrealism, he began to disarticulate figures. This was his 'Dinard' period ; then came that of the 'metamorphoses.' With Julio Gonzalez he made sculptures in wire and wrought-iron (ca. 1930) and he illustrated Ovid's *Metamorphoses* for Albert Skira (1931). Large retrospective exhibition of his work at the Georges Petit Gallery, Paris (1932). A trip to Spain resulted in his *Bull Fights* (1934). He wrote and published some Surrealist poetry in 1935. Next year he exhibited works in a new, strongly sculptural style ; in 1938 he began painting dislocated figures with double faces. He left Paris at the beginning of the war, but returned in 1940 and worked in seclusion on a synthetic expressionism of his own in which the

color suggests plastic relief. Since the war he has indulged in a variety of techniques. The bronze statue *Man with a Lamb* dates from 1945. Between 1945 and 1948 he produced a suite of over 60 lithographs, dazzling variations on a restricted number of motifs. At Vallauris in 1946 he developed an interest in ceramics. Painting again at Antibes (1946-1948) he created an imaginative mythology all his own in which flute-playing fauns play the leading part. Picasso today is still in full creative activity.

REGOYOS Y VALDES, DARIO DE (1857-1913).

Regoyos was the only Spanish painter to take an active part in the Impressionist movement. Born in the Asturias in 1857, he got his early training at the School of Fine Arts, Madrid, where in 1877 he was a pupil of the landscape-painter Haes. Going abroad, he stayed briefly in Paris, then moved to Brussels where in 1881 he struck up friendships with Meunier, Theo van Rysselberghe and Verhaeren ; in 1883 they all made a trip together to Spain, where Verhaeren wrote his *L'Espagne noire*, later illustrated by Regoyos. The artist joined ' Les Vingt,' a Brussels group which sponsored exhibitions of Degas, Whistler, Manet, Renoir, Sisley and Pissarro. Influenced above all by Pissarro, Regoyos himself painted in the Impressionist style and from time to time practiced a divisionist technique. In 1888 he made another trip to Spain with Verhaeren and at the end of the century he returned to his native country for good. He still painted a great deal, especially in northern Spain, in the Basque country, in the Asturias and in Catalonia, where he died in 1913.

RIBERA, JUSEPE (1591-1652).

His Italian biographers have many tales to tell of Ribera's stormy, picaresque career, and picture 'Lo Spagnoletto's ' life as an endless series of professional intrigues and rivalries, attempted poisonings due to *gelosia di mestiere*, conspiracies and brawls, triumphs and adversities, dramatic love affairs. Alternations of dark patches and dazzling light, glooms and raptures—just as in his painting. Perhaps we would do better to keep to the records and established dates of Ribera's life. He was born in 1591 at Jativa, hometown of the Borgias, in the province of Valencia. He was not of noble birth, as once was thought, but the son of a cobbler at Valencia. In that city he spent his 'prentice years as a painter and was Ribalta's pupil. He went to Italy as a young man, beginning with Rome, and passionately studied the great masters. Later, when his Spanish colleague Jusepe Martinez visited him at Naples in 1626, he spoke of his early passion for Raphael. He was also impressed by Michelangelo. But it was above all Caravaggio who opened his eyes and his influence on Ribera was decisive. Settling at Naples, where we find him married in 1616, Ribera soon made a name for himself, the Spanish Viceroy, the Duke of Osuna, taking him under his wing. He became Court Painter, appointed by the Duke and confirmed in this post by the Duke's successors. Orders flowed in and Ribera, with an apartment in the Palace, worked now only in the mornings and spent the rest of his time in society. Working under him in his studio were many young Neapolitan painters, among them Luca Giordano, the famous *Fa presto* and prodigious imitator, who turned out ' better ' Riberas than the master himself. Many distinctions came Ribera's way. In 1626 the Academy of Saint Luke in Rome elected him a member. Velazquez visited him in 1629 and bought pictures from him for Philip IV (he visited him again in 1649). In 1648 the Pope admitted him to the Military Order of Christ. It was now that his most celebrated works were gaining honored places in the world's museums : religious pictures, scenes of martyrdom, Magdalens, Immaculate Conceptions,

also his beggar-philosophers and his crippled, leering *lazzaroni*, tagged with Greek names and clad in rags and tatters. This, too, was a time of social unrest. Masaniello and the Neapolitan rabble launched a revolt against the Spaniards. Was Ribera in collusion with the rebels ? This seems very unlikely, even supposing his Italian disciples were involved. In any case, as a Spaniard and Court Painter he was on the best of terms with the man who put down the revolt, Don Juan of Austria, natural son of Philip IV. Ribera painted his portrait in 1648 and Don Juan haunted the painter's studio. Which led to a curious incident, little calculated to brighten Ribera's last years. The unscrupulous young nobleman, then nineteen, seduced the painter's sixteen-year-old daughter, Maria Rosa, and proceeded to abandon the girl, leaving her with two little daughters. In 1666 one of them, Ana Maria, entered the Convent of the ' Descalzas Reales ' in Madrid under the name of Sister Margarita de la Cruz. Don Juan was then minister to Charles II. Ribera died at Naples in 1652.

RIZI, FRAY JUAN (1600-1681) and FRANCISCO (1608-1685).

Contemporaries of Velazquez, but only very slightly influenced by his art, the Rizi brothers (Spanish on their mother's side) were the sons of Antonio Ricci, a painter from Bologna, who had worked at the Escorial. Juan was born in 1600. A youth of passionate disposition and full of religious fervor, he made a name for himself at sixteen, writing a precocious treatise on the Immaculate Conception, which he presented to Pope Paul V. Though immersed in philosophy and theology, he found time to study painting at the school of Juan Bautista Mayno. At twenty-seven he entered the Order of the Benedictines at Montserrat. For a while (1640) he was private tutor to the Infante Baltasar Carlos, but he never felt happy at the Royal Court and it was not long before he returned to the monastic life, and though for ever changing monasteries he painted indefatigably wherever he went. Nothing is known of his work prior to the great cycle of thirty pictures done in 1653, when the artist was already a middle-aged man, at San Milan de la Cogolla in the province of Rioja. These works are uneven as to their execution and their style is somber, combining rugged force with a certain uncouthness. Like Zurbaran (though there were no direct contacts between the two artists) Fray Juan Rizi was a ' painter of monks.' He also wrote a treatise on painting, *Pintura sabia*, for one of his pupils, the Duchess of Bejar, in which, curiously enough, among the sketches copiously illustrating the text we find a good many nudes, both male and female, drawn with remarkable care and delicacy. In the whole of Spanish art before Goya's time, the nude made but a single appearance : Velazquez' famous *Venus*, a picture which, however, he prudently kept at home and never exhibited. Fray Juan Rizi's career as a painter came to a close in 1662, when he moved first to Rome and then to the Monastery of Monte Cassino. He was about to be nominated Bishop when he died in 1681. His brother Francisco was a clever decorator in a style not devoid of brio. He had many pupils and left his mark on the tastes of the day, but his work suffered from careless, overhasty execution. He died in 1685, while working at the Escorial for Charles II.

ROSALES, EDUARDO (1836-1873).

Born in Madrid in 1836, Rosales spent his youth in extreme poverty whose effects permanently undermined his health and cut short his career at an early age. He began his art studies in 1851 at the Academy of Madrid and in 1857 went to Rome, where he laboriously groped for his way, trying his hand at academic and historical painting. His first success took place at the National Exhibition in Madrid (1864) and at the International Exhibition in Paris (1865). In 1871, still living in Rome, he sent in a large composition *The Death of Lucretia* (Museum of Modern Art, Madrid), in which, despite the academic theme, he displayed no little technical originality, combining vigor with an economy of means. He exhibited some remarkable portraits in this same year. At Murcia in his last years he also took to landscape-painting. He was appointed Director of the Spanish Academy in Rome in 1873, but died that same year in Madrid.

SOLANA, José GUTIERREZ. (1885-1945).

Born at Madrid in 1885 of an old Santander family, once of high social standing, Solana began painting when very young and did not study in the official schools, but worked alone driven on by a compelling sense of his own vocation. The only masters he acknowledged were Goya (especially the 'black paintings') and Brueghel. Although in Spain his painting has always been regarded as "peculiar" and a case apart, he did not lack official honor, and many exhibitions abroad gave him a worldwide reputation. Yet, right up to his death in 1945, his life was a gloomy, secluded one. Solana was also a writer and his *Scenes and Costumes of Madrid* (1912 and 1918), with its bitter, direct, often grotesque style, is like a description of his own paintings.

TRISTAN, Luis (1586?-1624).

This artist was El Greco's outstanding disciple at Toledo, in the neighborhood of which city he was born. His traditional (but unauthenticated) date of birth is 1586. What is certain is that he worked under El Greco from 1603 to 1607. The oldest pictures we have by Tristan date from 1613 : a *Beheading of St John the Baptist* (at the Carmelite Church, Toledo) and a *Holy Family* (in an Italian collection). In these El Greco's influence is oddly mingled with the boldest realism. The same ambiguous style, dominated by a strain of *tenebrismo* resembling that of such artists as Ribalta and Ribera, is present in his major works : the altarpiece in the Monastery of Yepes (1616) and that in Santa Clara at Toledo (1623). The excellent portrait of Archbishop Bernardo de Sandoval in the Toledo Cathedral (1619) is also by his hand, as are a considerable number of pictures both in Spain and abroad, among them an *Adoration of the Shepherds* (Cambridge Museum, 16 0) ; an *Adoration of the Kings* (Private Collection, New York, 1620) ; a *Pentecost* (Royal Gallery of Rumania), coming probably from the convent of the Queen's Nuns at Toledo ; and a *Trinity* (Cathedral of Seville, 1624). Tristan died at Toledo in 1624.

VALDÉS LEAL, JUAN DE (1622-1690).

Son of a Portuguese goldsmith and an Andalusian lady, Valdés Leal takes his place in the line of great half-Spanish, half-Portuguese painters that includes Sanchez Coello, Velazquez and Claudio Coello. Born at Seville in 1622, he spent most of his early years in Cordova where he studied under Antonio del Castillo and, in 1647, married a woman painter. His personality already asserted itself in his work at the Convent of the nuns of St Clare at Carmona in 1653-1654. Noteworthy in the outstanding picture of this group, *Attack of the Saracens on the Convent of St Francis* (now in the Museum of Seville), is the painter's excited handling of his theme, in which form is boldly and deliberately sacrificed to a baroque dynamism, sudden bursts of light and color. Records prove his presence at Seville in 1656, where he became Murillo's rival, executing among other works a cycle of pictures (1657-1658) illustrating the life of St Jerome, the most important of which (notably *The Temptation of St Jerome*) are now in the Museum of Seville, while others have found their way to the Prado and the Grenoble Museum. In 1658 he made a group of pictures in which his all-triumphant light and color reach their climax, for the high altar of the Carmelite Convent at Cordova. The *Assumption of Elias*, central picture of the group has been described as "a flame shooting up heavenwards." The artist himself was an aggressive, temperamental man who so outdistanced his Sevillian colleagues that when an Academy was founded at Seville in 1660 he was chosen major-domo. His crowning success came with two pictures he did in 1672 for the Church of the Hospital of La Caridad, in Seville : his curious allegories of *Death* and *Vanity* in which mediaeval asceticism is blended with macabre realism. He worked for many years at Seville and Cordova, and may have made a trip to Madrid in 1674. His last years mark a decline, and he was often aided by his son Lucas. The last picture signed by the artist is dated 1686. He died at Seville in 1690.

VELAZQUEZ, DIEGO DE SILVA Y (1599-1660).

With this great Spaniard the era of modern painting may be said to begin. Born at Seville in 1599 into a family of modest means which, Portuguese by origin, had been living in Andalusia for two generations, he began studying art when still young, to start with under Francisco Herrera the Elder, a good painter, but too harsh a taskmaster for the gentle, sensitive boy, and Velazquez was glad to leave him and join the studio of Francisco Pacheco, a less gifted, but more humane teacher. An artist of scholarly tastes, Pacheco saw to it that his pupil was well grounded in the rules of art, while Velazquez, striking out on his own lines, and working from nature, soon surpassed the level of instruction available at Seville. At nineteen he was the hope and pride of his master, whose daughter he now married. In 1622, making a bid for fortune, he went to Madrid, where he was well received by his fellow Sevillians at the Court and spent much time in the Prado and the Escorial. Though he was not given an opportunity of painting the King's portrait, he made that of Gongora, the poet. Presently he returned to Seville, confident that his day would come. And so it did the following year. Summoned to Madrid by Count-Duke Olivares, the all-powerful minister of the boy-king Philip IV, Velazquez was presented at the Palace by the great man himself and made a portrait of the King on horseback, in full armor. His triumph was complete : the picture was exhibited in a public square of the city, sonnets were written in the young painter's honor and the King at once enrolled him in his service. From now on, Velazquez' career was one of unbroken success, as artist, officer of the Court and soon as intimate friend of the King. In 1628 Rubens came to Madrid on a diplomatic mission. Velazquez was the only Spanish painter whom he sought out and cultivated. The two artists soon became good friends and went together to the Escorial to see the royal collections. Their talks revived Velazquez' desire to make a study trip to Italy and next year, as a reward for his picture *The Topers*, the King gave him permission to go abroad. At Venice he copied Tintoretto and bought pictures for the King ; passing by way of Ferrara, he went to Rome where he stayed a full year, studying Michelangelo and Raphael at the Vatican. During this period he painted *Joseph's Coat* and the *Forge of Vulcan*. He went as far as Naples, where he met Ribera, and then turned his steps homeward, as King Philip was fretting at the absence of his favorite painter. Now came the period of that imposing series of portraits which have immortalized the Spanish Court of that day (Philip IV, the Infante Baltasar Carlos, Don Fernando and Don Carlos, the King's brothers, and his sister, Queen Maria of Hungary and Count-Duke Olivares) and historical pictures such as *The Surrender of*

Breda—each a masterpiece of monumental grandeur and striking lifelikeness. In 1648 Velazquez made a second trip to Italy, whither he was sent by the King to purchase works of art and to seek out painters for the Alcazar at Madrid. He saw Venice again, traveled to Parma and Florence, and at Naples paid another visit to Ribera, his countryman, who was now at the summit of his fame and on the brink of those misfortunes which clouded his last years. He made a long stay in Rome, lionized and heaped with honors at the Court of Innocent X, painting his great portrait of this Pope and ordering pictures from Poussin and some of the Roman painters. He had intended to return to Spain by way of Paris, but war conditions forced him to abandon this project. Returning via Genoa, he was back in Madrid in 1651, after a three years' absence. Though his artistic powers were now at their height, the last years of his life saw a slowing down in his output, as his official duties at the Court were becoming more onerous. The King lavished favors on him, honored him with the post of Grand Marshall of the Palace, which obliged the painter to busy himself with the thousand and one futilities and outward shows of a Court punctilious to the extreme. All kindness and compliancy, Velazquez deferred to the whims of the aging, unhappy monarch who, in an effort to dispel his melancholy, surrounded himself with dwarfs and jesters whom he charged the painter to depict. Though taken up with portraits of this kind, he yet found time to finish a few last great works, among them *Las Meninas*, that marvel of technique and subtle effects, and *The Spinners*, a masterpiece revealing Velazquez as one of the pioneers of Impressionism. But the strain of the multifarious activities imposed by his official duties had told on him. In 1660 there took place, on the frontier of the Pyrenees, the presentation of the Infanta Maria Teresa to Louis XIV, her husband-to-be, and the entire Spanish Court moved from Madrid to Irun for the occasion. As Grand Marshal of the Palace Velazquez was responsible for all the travel preparations of the royal-party and for the elaborate ceremonies at the frontier. All went smoothly, the two Kings met in a sumptuous setting and the artist himself cut a notable figure at the ceremony. But the effort had overtaxed his strength. He had a break-down and abruptly died in Madrid. His wife survived him by only one week.

ZULOAGA Y ZABALETA, IGNACIO (1870-1945).

Of Basque extraction, he was born at Eibar in 1870 into a family of engravers and ceramists. He studied at Rome, but only found his feet in Paris after 1900, when he had much success with his Spanish themes and his portraits, among them *Maurice Barrès* (De Besteigui Collection, Bordeaux) and *La Comtesse de Noailles* (Museum of Bilbao). He later adopted a more somber palette, with a liberal use of black,

but only to swing back to a range of brilliant colors. Zuloaga was a great admirer of El Greco. He died in Madrid, in 1945.

ZURBARAN, FRANCISCO (1598-1664).

Zurbaran was born into a peasant family at Fuente de Cantos, a small village in Estremadura, in 1598. When still a boy, he was sent to Seville by his parents to study painting. At sixteen he was the pupil of an obscure Sevillian painter of whom we know no more than the name, Pedro Diaz de Villanueva, and with whom he made great strides. Two years later, in 1616, the young artist signed a *Purisima* in which his exceptional gifts were apparent. At twenty, he quit Seville for Llerena in Estremadura, where he married and settled for a time. 1628 saw him back in Seville; his reputation seems to have grown, for he at once set to work executing commissions in the Convents of La Merced (" Our Lady of Ransom ," patroness of the religious Order whose mission was the ransoming of Christian captives) and San Pablo. Thus he started his career as a painter of the monastic life, exalting the asceticism of the cloistered life and the practices of sainthood. His abilities won him speedy recognition and from the following year on, with the backing of some of the leading notables of the city, steps were taken to appoint him official painter of Seville. He obtained this post, although the local artists, headed by Alonso Cano, protested vigorously. But Zurbaran's star was in the ascendant; his fame spread to Madrid and the King invited him to do a series of pictures for his new palace of Buen Retiro. The subject imposed on him for these paintings *(The Labors of Hercules)* obviously went counter to the artist's personality. During these very years 1638-1639, he reverted to his true vocation, religious painting, and produced some of his major works, the two cycles of pictures at the Church of Guadalupe and the Carthusian Monastery of Jerez. Henceforth Zurbaran divided his time between Seville and Madrid. But meanwhile it would seem that something occurred which disastrously affected the artist's life : his painting began to lose its driving force, while his personality slowly disintegrated. What it was that led to this decline—whether illness, family troubles, the loss of his first wife in 1639, or the meteoric rise to fame of Murillo, who was hailed as a more typical representative of the Andalusian School—has never been satisfactorily determined. Quite possibly Zurbaran was galled by the success of his new rival; the painting of his last period certainly betrays the somewhat deleterious influence of Murillo. We find him at Madrid in 1658, when he made a declaration in favor of his friend Velazquez and was employed in the Convent of Atocha. No further mention of him is extant, though he is known to have been alive in 1664. After patient research Maria Luisa Caturla has fixed his death as having taken place on August 27, 1664.

BIBLIOGRAPHY

For books by Early Writers, Modern Texts and Documentation, and General Works, see under these headings in our first volume of SPANISH PAINTING, *From the Catalan Frescos to El Greco*, page 133. As was stated there, this Bibliography, with a few exceptions, is confined to works that have appeared in book form.

XVIIth CENTURY

W. WEISSBACH, *Der Barock als Kunst der Gegenreformation*, Berlin 1921. W. WEISSBACH, *Spanish Baroque Art*, Cambridge 1941. E. LAFUENTE, *La pintura española del siglo XVII* (Historia del Arte ' Labor,' vol. XII), Barcelona 1935 ; 2nd ed. 1945. N. SENTENACH, *La pintura en Madrid desde sus orígenes al siglo XIX*, Boletín de la Real Acad. de Hist., vol. XVI, Madrid 1910. A. DE BERUETE, *The School of Madrid*, London-New York 1911. F. J. SANCHEZ CANTON, *Los pintores de cámara de los reyes de España*, Bol. de la Soc. Esp. de Exc., vol. XXI-XXII, Madrid 1914-1915. E. TORMO, *En las Descalzas Reales*, Madrid 1917. E. TORMO, *Las iglesias del antiguo Madrid*, Madrid 1927, 2 vols. L. TRAMOYERES, *Un colegio de pintores. Documentos inéditos para la Historia del Arte en Valencia en el siglo XVII*, Valencia 1912. L. TRAMOYERES, *El realismo en la pintura valenciana del siglo XVII*, Valencia 1941. M. GOMEZ MORENO, *Guia de Granada*, Granada 1942. F. B. SAN ROMAN, *Noticias nuevas para la biografía del pintor Luis Tristán*, Toledo 1924. A. ARAGONÉS, *Tristán y Velázquez*, Toledo 1925. L. TRAMOYERES, *El pintor Jerónimo Jacinto de Espinosa en el Museo de Valencia*, Valencia 1916. E. OROZCO DIAZ, *Pedro Anastasio Bocanegra*, Granada 1937. E. OROZCO DIAZ, *Ambrosio Martinez de Bustos, pintor y poeta*, Granada 1936. F. J. SANCHEZ CANTON, *Dibujos españoles, IV. Alonso Cano*, Madrid, n. d. M. GOMEZ MORENO, *Alonso Cano*, Granada, n. d. E. TORMO, *Un gran pintor vallisoletano : Antonio de Pereda*, Valladolid 1916. B. BERJANO ESCOBAR, *D. Juan Carreño de Miranda*, Madrid 1924. E. TORMO, *La vida y la obra de Fray Juan Ricci ; Biografía del pintor D. Juan Andrés Ricci, monje de Montserrat*, by P. Celestino Gusi ; *Textos y juicios críticos sobre Fr. Juan Ricci con el Tratado de la Pintura sabia del P. Ricci*. Edition prepared by E. Lafuente-Ferrari, Madrid 1930, 2 vols. J. ALLENDE SALAZAR, *Antoliñez, pintor madrileño*, Bol. de la Soc. Esp. de Exc., vol. XXIII, Madrid 1916. L. ESCRIBANO, *Breve reseña biográfica del célebre pintor D. Acisclo Antonio Palomino*, Madrid 1859. E. MOYA, *El magno pintor del empíreo, D. Antonio Palomino de Castro*, Melilla 1928. P. GARIN, *Loa y elegía de Palomino*, Valencia 1941. J. CAVESTAN, *Floreros y bodegones en la pintura española. Catálogo de la Exposición de Amigos del Arte*, Madrid 1936-1940.

RIBERA

A. L. MAYER, *Jusepe de Ribera*, Leipzig 1908, 2nd ed. 1923. P. LAFOND, *Ribera et Zurbaran*, Paris 1909. M. UTRILLO, *Ribera el Españoleto*, Barcelona 1918. E. TORMO, *Ribera en el Museo del Prado*, Barcelona (Coll. ' El Arte en España ') 1923. J. SANTAMARINA, *Ribera*, Barcelona (Bibl. de Arte Hispánico) 1942. B. DE PANTORBA, *Ribera*, Barcelona, coll. ' Iberia,' n. d.

ZURBARAN

C. VINEGRA, *Catálogo ilustrado de la exposición de obras de Zurbarán*, Madrid 1905. E. TORMO, *El monasterio de Guadalupe y los cuadros de Zurbarán*, Madrid 1906. P. LAFOND, *Ribera et Zurbaran*, Paris 1909. J. CASCALES Y MUÑOZ, *Francisco de Zurbarán. Su época, su vida y sus obras*, Madrid 1911, 2nd ed. 1931 (English ed., New York 1918). MARTIN S. SORIA, *Francisco de Zurbaran. A Study of his Style*, Gazette des Beaux-Arts, 1944. F. J. SANCHEZ CANTON, *La sensibilidad de Zurbarán*, Granada 1944. M. L. CATURLA, *Zurbarán en el Salón de Reinos*, Arch. Esp. de Arte, 1945. P. GUINARD, *Los conjuntos dispersos o desaparecidos de Zurbarán. Anotaciones a Ceán Bermudez*, Arch. Esp. de Arte, 1937. F. POMPEY, *Zurbarán*, Madrid 1947. J. A. GAYA NUÑO, *Zurbarán*, Barcelona 1948. B. DE PANTORBA, *Zurbarán*, Barcelona, coll. ' Iberia,' n. d.

MURILLO

DAVIES, *The Life of Esteban Murillo, compiled from the writings of various authors*, London 1819. SCOTT, *Murillo and the Spanish School of Painting*, London 1863. F. M. TUBINO, *Murillo. Su época, su vida, sus cuadros*, Seville 1864. STROMER, *Murillo, Leben und Werke*, Berlin 1879. Ch. B. CURTIS, *Velazquez, and Murillo*, London-New York 1883. L. ALFONSO, *Murillo, El hombre, el artista, las obras*, Barcelona 1883. K. JUSTI, *Murillo*, Leipzig 1892. P. LEFORT, *Murillo et ses élèves*, Paris 1892. KNACKFUSS, *Murillo*, Leipzig 1899. P. LAFOND, *Murillo*, Paris 1907. A. L. MAYER, *Murillo*, Stuttgart and Berlin 1913. A. L. MAYER, *Murillo* (Klassiker der Kunst, vol. 22), Berlin and Leipzig, 2nd ed. 1923. J. DE LA VEGA, *Murillo*, Seville 1921. S. MONTOTO, *Bartolomé Esteban Murillo, Estudio biográfico crítico*, Seville 1923. A. VEGUE, *El sevillanismo de Murillo* (Temas de Arte y Literatura), Madrid 1928. S. MONTOTO, *Murillo*, Barcelona 1932. A. MUÑOZ, *Murillo*, Rome 1941. E. M. AGUILERA, *Murillo*, Barcelone, coll. ' Iberia,' n. d.

VALDÉS LEAL

C. LOPEZ MARTINEZ, *Valdés Leal y sus discípulos*, Seville 1907. A. DE BERUETE, *Valdés Leal*, Madrid 1911. J. GESTOSO PEREZ, *Biografía del pintor D. Juan de Valdés Leal*, Seville 1917. C. LOPEZ MARTINEZ, *Valdés Leal*, Seville 1922. A. GUICHOT, *Los famosos jeroglíficos de la Muerte de Juan de Valdés Leal de 1672. Estudio crítico*, Seville 1930.

VELAZQUEZ

W. STIRLING, *Velazquez et ses œuvres. Avec des notes et Catalogue des tableaux de Velazquez, par W. Bürger*, Paris 1865. Baron Ch. DAVILLIER, *Mémoire de Velazquez*, Paris 1874. Ch. B. CURTIS, *Velazquez and Murillo*, London-New York 1883. G. CRUZADA VILLAMIL, *Anales de la vida y de las obras de Diego de Silva Velázquez*, Madrid 1885. K. JUSTI, *Diego Velazquez und sein Jahrhundert*, Bonn 1888 ; and 1903, 1921, 1933. K. JUSTI, *Velazquez and his Times*, London 1889. P. LEFORT, *Velazquez*, Paris 1888. P. LEPRIEUR, *Velazquez*, Paris 1888. R. STEVENSON, *Velazquez*, London 1895. V. ARMSTRONG, *Velazquez, A Study of his Life and Art*, London 1897. KNACKFUSS, *Velazquez*, Leipzig 1898. I. O. PICON, *Vida y obras de D. Diego Velazquez*, Madrid 1898, 2nd ed. 1925. M. MESONERO ROMANOS, *Velázquez fuera del Museo del Prado*, Madrid 1899. A. BERUETE, *Velazquez*, Paris 1899 ; London 1906 ; Berlin 1909. E. SERRANO FATIGATI, *Bibliografía de Velázquez*, Rev. de Archivos, Madrid 1899. K. VALL, *Velazquez*, Munich 1899. E. FAURE, *Velazquez*, Paris 1903. A. BREAL, *Velazquez*, London 1905. J. R. MELIDA, *Los Velazquez de la casa Villahermosa*, Madrid 1905. GENSEL, *Velazquez*, Stuttgart-Leipzig, 1905. P. LAFOND, *Velazquez*, Paris 1906. A. L. MAYER, *Kleine Velazquez-Studien*, Munich 1913. AMAN-JEAN, *Velazquez*, Paris 1913. BERUETE, hijo, *Velázquez en el Museo del Prado*, Barcelona 1914. E. TORMO, *Velázquez. L'œuvre du maître*, Paris 1914. H. KEHRER, *Velazquez*, Leipzig 1919. MORENO VILLA, *Velázquez*, Madrid 1920. A. L. MAYER, *Diego Velazquez*, Berlin 1923. ALLENDE-SALAZAR, *Velazquez*, Klassiker der Kunst, Stuttgart, 4th ed. 1925. A. L. MAYER, *Velazquez. A Catalogue Raisonné of the Pictures and*

Drawings, London 1936. A. L. MAYER, *Velazquez*, Paris 1941. A. MUÑOZ, *Velazquez*, Rome 1941. F. J. SANCHEZ CANTON, *Como vivia Velazquez*, Arch. Esp. de Arte 1942. E. LAFUENTE, *Velazquez. Introduction. Catalogue*, Oxford 1943. F. J. SANCHEZ CANTON, *Las Meninas y sus personages*, Barcelona 1943. E. LAFUENTE, *Velazquez* (Biblioteca de Arte Hispánico), Barcelona 1944. D. ANGULO IÑIGUEZ, *Como Velazquez compuso sus cuadros*, Séville (Laboratorio de Arte de la Universidad de S.) 1947. E. DU GUE TRAPIER, *Velazquez*. The Hispanic Society of America, New York 1948. F. J. SANCHEZ CANTON, *La librería de Velázquez*, in ' Homenaje a R. Menéndez Pidal,' vol. III. L. P. FARGUE, *Velazquez*, Paris, ' Les Demi-Dieux.' R. BENET, *Velázquez*, Barcelona, coll. ' Iberia', n. d. ORTEGA Y GASSET, *Papeles de Velázquez y de Goya*, Madrid 1951.

XVIIIth CENTURY

ANTONIO RAFAEL MENGS, *Obras de...*, edited by José Nicolas de Azura, Madrid 1780. J. FABRE, *Descripción de las alegorias pintadas en las bovedas del Real Palacio de Madrid*, Madrid 1829. CAVEDA, *Memorias para la historia de la Real Academia de San Fernando*, Madrid 1867. J. FONTANALS DEL CASTILLO, *Antonio Viladomat*, Barcelona 1877. R. BENET, *Viladomat*, Barcelona, coll. ' Iberia', n. d. R. ROS, *Los frescos del Pilar en Zaragosa*, Huesca 1904. F. J. SANCHEZ CANTON, *Mengs en España*, Madrid 1927. F. J. SANCHEZ CANTON, *Antonio Rafael Mengs*, Madrid 1929. E. TORMO, *La visita a las colecciones artísticas de la Real Academia de San Fernando*, Madrid 1929. E. LAFUENTE, *Grabados y dibujos de Tiepolo*, Madrid 1935. E. M. AGUILERA, *Pintores españoles del siglo XVIII*, Barcelona, coll. 'Iberia', n. d.

GOYA

Laurent MATHERON, *Goya*, Paris 1858. Ch. IRIARTE, *Goya. La biographie, les fresques, les toiles, les tapisseries, les eaux-fortes et le catalogue de l'œuvre*, Paris 1867. F. ZAPATER, *Goya. Noticias biográficas*, Saragossa 1868 (reprinted in the magazine ' Universidad ', Saragossa 1928 and in the volume *Goya*, ed. by Calleja, Madrid 1924). G. CRUZADA VILLAMIL, *Los tapices de Goya*, Madrid 1870. P. LEFORT, *Francisco Goya*, Paris 1877. Count of VIÑAZA, *Goya*, Madrid 1887. J. DE LA RADA Y DELGADO, *Frescos de Goya en la iglesia de San Antonio de la Florida*, Madrid 1888. Z. ARAUJO, *Goya*, Madrid 1895. E. TORMO, *Desarrollo de la pintura española del siglo XVIII. Las pinturas de Goya y su clasificación cronológica*, Madrid 1902. V. VON LOGA, *Francisco Goya*, Berlin 1903. J. R. MELIDA, *Goya y la pintura contemporanea*, Madrid 1906. P. BEROQUI, *Goya, pintor de retratos*, Madrid 1906. V. VON LOGA, *Goyas seltene Radierungen u. Lithographien*, Berlin 1907. P. LAFOND, *Goya*, Paris 1907. R. OERTEL, *Goya*, Leipzig 1907. A. F. CALVAERT, *Goya*, London 1908. ACCHIARDI, *Les dessins de D. F. de Goya au Musée du Prado*, Rome 1908. H. STOKES, *Goya*. London 1914. F. BOIX, *Los dibujos de Goya*, Madrid 1922. *Goya, Cuadros y dibujos*, Madrid, Calleja, 1924. A. L. MAYER, *Francisco de Goya*, Barcelona 1925. A. GASCON DE GOTOR, *Goya, pintor de Historia*, Saragossa 1926. R. DEL ARCO, *Por qué Goya pintó como pintó*, Saragossa 1926. A. DE BERUETE, *Francisco Goya*, Madrid 1928. P. FREDERIX, *Goya*, Paris 1928. B. DE PANTORBA, *Goya*, Madrid 1928. JUAN DE LA ENCINA, *Goya en zig-zag, Bosquejo de interpretación biográfica*, Madrid 1928. E. LAFUENTE and J. ALLENDE-SALAZAR, *Catalogo ilustrado de la Exposición de pinturas de Goya. Museo del Prado*, Madrid 1928. J. EZQUERRA DEL BAYO, *La duquesa de Alba y Goya*, Madrid 1928. F. J. SANCHEZ CANTON, *Goya en la Academia*, Madrid 1928. C. PEMAN, *Los Goyas de Cádiz*, Cadiz 1928. F. J. SANCHEZ CANTON, *Museo del Prado, Goya*, Madrid, I, 1928 ; II, 1941. F. J.

SANCHEZ CANTON, *Goya*, Paris 1930. C. TERRASSE, *Goya*, Paris 1931. G. GRAPPE, *Goya*, Paris 1937. CARDERERA, *Goya*, Madrid 1939. A. SALCEDO, *La época de Goya*, Madrid, n. d. D. CATTON RICH and F. SCHMID, *The Art of Francisco Goya*, The Art Institute of Chicago 1941. Eugenio D'ORS, *Epos de los destinos. Goya*, Madrid 1943. X. DE SALAS, *La familia de Carlos IV* (Obras maestras del Arte español) Barcelona 1944. H. ROTHE, *Las pinturas del Panteon de Goya (San Antonio de la Florida)*, Barcelona 1944. A. L. MAYER, *Die Skizzenbücher Francisco Goyas*, Berlin n. d. E. M. AGUILERA, *Las pinturas negras de Goya*, Madrid, n. d. D. SANCHEZ RIVERA, *Goya. La enfermedad, la leyenda negra y las pinturas religiosas*, Madrid 1945. Dr. BLANCO SOLER, *Goya, su infermedad y su arte*, Madrid 1947. A. RUIZ CABRIADA, *Bibliografia de Goya*, Madrid 1946. E. D'ORS, *Vie de Goya*, Paris 1928. E. D'ORS, *El arte de Goya*, Madrid 1946. (Patrimonio Nacional - Palacio de Oriente), *Catálogo de la Exposición commemorativa del centenario de Goya*, Madrid 1946. V. DE SAMBRICIO, *Tapices de Goya*, Madrid 1946. I. DE BERYES, *Dibujos y grabados de Goya*, Barcelona, coll. ' Iberia ', n. d. J. LASSAIGNE, *Goya*, Paris 1946. André MALRAUX, *Dessins de Goya au Musée du Prado*, Geneva 1947. E. LAFUENTE FERRARI, *Antecedentes, coincidencias y influencias del arte de Goya*, Madrid 1947. A. VALLENTIN, *Goya*, Paris 1951. F. J. SANCHEZ CANTON, *Vida y obras de Goya*, Madrid 1951. ORTEGA Y GASSET, *Papeles de Velazquez y de Goya*, Madrid 1951. NUÑEZ DE ARENAS, *Le Sort de Goya en France*, Bordeaux 1951.

XIXth CENTURY

M. OSSORIO BERNARD, *Galeria biográfica de artistas españoles del siglo XIX*, Madrid, 1st ed., 2 vols. 1868-1869 ; 2nd ed., I vol. 1883-1884. A. G. TEMPLE, *Modern Spanish Painting*, London 1908. A. DE BERUETE, *Historia de la pintura española del siglo XIX*, Madrid 1926. M. ABRIL, *La pintura española del siglo XIX*, (appendix to the IVth vol. of *Historia del Arte* by Woermann, Madrid 1926). Sociedad Española de Amigos del Arte, *Catálogo de la Exposición de pintura española de la primera mitad del siglo XIX*, Madrid 1913. Sociedad Española de Amigos del Arte, *Exposición de dibujos espanoles, 1750-1860*, by F. BOIX, Madrid 1922. Elizabeth DU GUE TRAPIER, *The Hispanic Society of America, Catalogue of Paintings (19th and 20th Centuries)*, New York 1932. E. M. AGUILERA, *Vicente Lopez*, Barcelona, coll. ' Iberia ', n. d. M. DE LOZOYA, *Vicente Lopez, 1772-1850, Catálogo de la Exposición organizada por los Amigos de los Museos de Barcelona*, Barcelona 1943. M. DE MADRAZO, *Federico de Madrazo*, coll. ' Estrella ', Madrid, 2 vols., n. d. A. MENDEZ CASALS, *Jenaro Perez Villamil*, Madrid, coll. ' La Esfinge ', n. d. B. DE PANTORBA, *Los Madrazos*, Barcelona, coll. ' Iberia ', n. d. C. PALENCIA, *Leonardo Alenza*, Madrid, coll. ' Estrella ', n. d. J. LAZARO, *Les deux Lucas*, Paris 1936. Elizabeth DU GUE TRAPIER, *Eugenio Lucas y Padilla*, New York 1940. J. A. GAYA NUÑO, *Eugenio Lucas*, Barcelona, n. d. B. DE PANTORBA, *Eduardo Rosales*, Madrid 1937. E. M. AGUILERA, *Rosales*, Barcelona, coll. , Iberia ', n. d. F. JIMENEZ-PLACER, *La pintura española en la época del realismo y del impresionismo* (in *Historia del Arte ' Labor '*, vol. XV), Barcelona 1944. Baron DAVILLIER, *Fortuny ; sa vie, son œuvre, sa correspondance*, Paris 1875. Ch. IRIARTE, *Fortuny*, Paris 1886. *Sociedad de Amigos de los Museos, Catálogo de la Exposición Fortuny*, Barcelona 1940. A. OFISSO, *Arte y artistas catalanes*, Barcelona 1900. J. F. RAFOLS, *El arte modernista en Barcelona*, Barcelona 1943. J. PLA, *Rusiñol y su tiempo*, Barcelona 1943. M. ABRIL, *Ramon Casas*, Madrid, coll. ' Estrella ', n. d. B. DE PANTORBA, *El paisaje y los paisajistas españoles*, Madrid 1943. B. DE PANTORBA, *Meyfren*, Barcelona 1942. J. PLA, *El pintor Joaquin Mir*, Barcelona 1944. J. MATES, *El pintor Gimeno*, Sabadell 1935. M. ABRIL, *Sorolla*, Barcelona, coll. ' Iberia ', n. d. B. DE PANTORBA, *Sorolla*, Gerona 1944.

XXth CENTURY

M. ABRIL, *De la Naturaleza al Espíritu. Ensayo crítico de pintura contemporanea desde Sorolla a Picasso*, Madrid 1930. Eugenio D'ORS, *Mis Salones. Itinerario histórico del Arte moderno en la capital de España*, Madrid 1945. *Maestros de la pintura moderna* (Beruete, Gimeno, Echevarría, Iturrino, Regoyos, Nonell, Pidelaserra, Solana), Madrid, coll. ' Cariatide ', 1952. L.-F. VIVANCO, *Primera Bienal Hispano-Americana de Arte*, Madrid 1952. Dario DE REGOYOS, *La España Negra de Verhaeren*, Barcelona 1899. R. SORIANO, *Dario de Regoyos*, Madrid 1921. R. BENET, *Regoyos*, Barcelona, coll. ' Iberia ', n. d. I. DE BERYES, *Zuloaga*, Barcelona, coll. ' Iberia ', n. d. E. LAFUENTE, *La vida y el arte de Ignacio Zuloaga*, San Sebastian 1950. A. DEL CASTILLO, *José Maria Sert*, Barcelona 1947. R. BENET, *Nonell*, Barcelona, coll. ' Iberia ', n. d. José G. SOLANA, *Madrid. Escenas y costumbres*, Madrid, vol. 1, 1913 ; vol. 2, 1918. C. BARBERAN, *Gutierrez Solana*, Madrid 1933. Ramon GOMEZ DE LA SERNA, *José Gutierrez Solana*, Buenos-Ayres, 1944. E. M. AGUILERA, *Solana*, Barcelona, coll. ' Iberia ', n. d. M. SANCHEZ CAMARGO, *José Gutierrez Solana*, Madrid 1946. L. GIL FILLIOL, *Vázquez Díaz*, Barcelona, coll., ' Iberia ', n. d. J. A. GAYA NUÑO, *Francisco Cossia*, Madrid 1951. Benjamin PALENCIA, *Palabras*, Madrid 1932.

PICASSO

G. APOLLINAIRE, *Les peintres cubistes*, Paris 1913. G. COQUIOT, *Cubistes, futuristes, passéistes*, Paris 1914. A. SALMON, *La jeune peinture française*, Paris 1917. J. MEIER-GRAEFE, *Entwicklungsgeschichte der Modernen Kunst*, Munich 1914. W. GEORGE, *Picasso*, Paris 1924. M. Raynal, *Les maîtres du cubisme*, Paris 1921. M. RAYNAL, *Pablo Picasso*, Paris, by L'Effort Moderne, 1921 ; German ed. 1921. M. RAYNAL, *Picasso*, Paris, by Crès 1922. J. COCTEAU, *Picasso*, Paris 1923. P. REVERDY, *Picasso*, Paris 1926. A. BRETON, *Le Surréalisme et la peinture*, Paris 1928. W. UHDE, *Picasso et la tradition française*, Paris 1929 ; English ed., New York 1929. ARAGON, *La peinture au défi*, Paris 1930. H. MAHAUT, *Picasso*, Paris 1930. C. ZERVOS, *Picasso*, vol. I (1895-1906), vol. II in two parts (1906-1912 and 1912-1917), Paris, by Cahiers d'Art 1932-1942. B. GEISER, *Picasso, peintre-graveur*. Illustrated catalog of his engravings and lithographs, 1899-1931, Bern 1933. E. D'ORS, *La vie de Picasso*, Paris 1930 ; English ed. 1934. *Cahiers d'Art*, Special numbers on Picasso : 3/5 (1932) ; 7/10 (1935) ; 4/5 (1937) ; 3/10 (1938) ; 1940-1944, numbers on Picasso ; 1948, number on Picasso's Ceramics. A. H. BARR, *Cubism and Abstract Art*, New York, Museum of Modern Art 1936. Fernande OLIVIER, *Picasso et ses amis*, Paris 1934. Gertrude STEIN, *Picasso*, Paris 1938. J. CASSOU, *Picasso*, Paris 1940. J. SABARTÈS, *Picasso, portraits et souvenirs*, Paris 1946 ; English ed., New York 1948. *Couleur de Picasso*, special number of ' Verve ', Paris

1948. D. SUTTON, *Picasso, époques bleue et rose*, Paris 1948. E. D'ORS, *El arte de Picasso*, Madrid 1945. A. H. BARR, *Picasso, Fifty Years of his Art*, New York, Museum of Modern Art, 1946. B. GEISER, *Pablo Picasso. Lithographs 1945-1948*, New York 1948. C. ZERVOS, *Dessins de Picasso*, Paris 1949. S. and G. RAMIÉ, *Céramiques de Picasso*, Geneva 1948 ; English ed., 1950. J. LASSAIGNE, *Picasso*, Paris 1950. A. CIRICI-PELLICER, *Picasso avant Picasso*, Geneva 1950.

JUAN GRIS

G. APOLLINAIRE, *Les peintres cubistes*, Paris 1913. M. RAYNAL, *Juan Gris*, Paris 1920. D. H. KAHNWEILER, *Juan Gris* (Junge Kunst. 55), Leipzig 1926. C. ZERVOS, *Juan Gris et l'inquiétude d'aujourd'hui*, in *Cahiers d'Art*, No. 10, Paris 1926. E. TÉRIADE, *Juan Gris*, in *Cahiers d'art*, No. 5-6, Paris 1928. W. GEORGE, *Juan Gris*, Paris 1931. *Cahiers d'Art*, No. 5-6, Paris 1933. Number devoted to Juan Gris. (Articles by Daniel Henry, Juan Gris, Apollinaire, Raynal, Ozenfant, Zervos, etc.). Gertrude STEIN, *The Life of Juan Gris*, New York 1935. A. H. BARR, *Cubism and Abstract Art*. New York 1936. D. H. KAHNWEILER, *Juan Gris. Sa vie et son œuvre*, Paris 1946 (fully documented) English ed., London 1947.

MIRO

A. BRETON, *Le surréalisme et la peinture*, Paris 1928 ; 2nd ed., New York 1945. SALVADOR DALI, *Joan Miro*, in *L'Amic de les Arts*, Sitges 1928. D. GASCOYNE, *A Short Survey of Surrealism*, London 1935. A. H. BARR, *Fantastic Art, Dada and Surrealism*, New York, Museum of Modern Art, 1936. J. LEVY, *Surrealism*, New York 1936. J. J. SWEENEY, *Joan Miro*, New York, Museum of Modern Art 1941 (with bibliography). A. CIRICI-PELLICER, *Miro y la imaginación*, Barcelona 1949. I.-E. CIRLOT, *Joan Miro*, Barcelona 1949.

DALI

R. CREVEL, *Dali ou l'antiobscurantisme*, Paris 1931. J. LACAN, *De la psychose paranoïaque dans ses rapports avec la personnalité*, Paris 1932. M. BLOCK, *Salvador Dali*, in ' Current Biography ' 1940 (with bibliography). A. BRETON, *Le surréalisme et la peinture*, New York 1945. J. Th. SOBY, *Salvador Dali*, New York, Museum of Modern Art, 1946 (with bibliography). Dr. A. ORIOL ANGUERA, *Salvador Sali*, Barcelona 1949. Ana Maria DALI, *S. Dali visto por su hermana*, Barcelona 1949. J. A. GAYA NUÑO, *Salvador Dali*, Barcelona 1952. R. SANTOS TORROELLA, *Salvador Dali*, Madrid 1952. Works by Dali : *La femme visible*, Paris 1930 ; *Conquest of the Irrational*, New York 1935; *Declaration of the Independence of the Imagination and the Rights of Man to his own Madness*, New York 1939; *The Secret of Life of Salvador Dali*, New York 1941; *50 Secrets of Magic Craftsmanship*, New York 1948.

INDEX OF NAMES